DAVID FLANDERS

ACCOUNTING
TO TRIAL BALANCE AND BASIC REPORTS

WORKBOOK

6

DISK INCLUDED
WITH UWATCH DEMONSTRATIONS
AND ADDITIONAL EXERCISES

Accounting Workbook: To Trial Balance and Basic Reports
6th Edition
David Flanders

Publishing manager: Dorothy Chiu
Senior publishing editor: Sophie Kaliniecki
Developmental editor: Tharaha Richards
Project editor: Michaela Skelly
Art direction: Olga Lavecchia
Cover designer: Leigh Ashforth
Editor: Diane Fowler

Any URLs contained in this publication were checked for currency during the production process. Note, however, that the publisher cannot vouch for the ongoing currency of URLs.

The 5th edition was published in 2011

© 2015 Cengage Learning Australia Pty Limited

For product information and technology assistance,
in Australia call **1300 790 853**;
in New Zealand call **0800 449 725**

For permission to use material from this text or product, please email
aust.permissions@cengage.com

National Library of Australia Cataloguing-in-Publication Data
Author: Flanders, David
Title: *Accounting Workbook: To Trial Balance and Basic Reports*
             David Flanders.
Edition: 6th edition
ISBN: 9780170245524 (loose-leaf)
Subjects: Accounting.
             Accounting--Problems, exercises, etc.
Dewey number: 657.044

Cengage Learning Australia
Level 7, 80 Dorcas Street
South Melbourne, Victoria Australia 3205

Cengage Learning New Zealand
Unit 4B Rosedale Office Park
331 Rosedale Road, Albany, North Shore 0632, NZ

For learning solutions, visit **cengage.com.au**

Printed in China by 1010 Printing International Limited.
7 8 9 10 11 12 24 23

ACCOUNTING
TO TRIAL BALANCE

WORKBOOK

DISK INCLUDED
WITH UWATCH DEMONSTRATIONS
AND ADDITIONAL EXERCISES

Ex. 1.1   **Briefly outline the meaning of the term 'accounting'.**

_____

_____

_____

_____

Ex. 1.2   **What is a business? Discuss.**

_____

_____

_____

_____

_____

Ex. 1.3   **Briefly describe the three common types of business ownership.**

Sole Trader

_____

_____

Partnership

_____

_____

Company

_____

_____

Ex. 1.4   **Difference between public and a private company limited by shares.**

Public company

_____

_____

_____

_____

Private company limited by shares

_____

_____

_____

_____

Ex. 1.5   Solution in textbook.
            Advantages and disadvantages of the common forms of business ownership.

Advantages of being a sole trader

_____
_____

Disadvantages of being a sole trader

_____
_____

Advantages of being in a partnership

_____
_____

Disadvantages of being a partnership

_____
_____
_____
_____

Advantages of being a company

_____
_____
_____
_____
_____

Disadvantages of being a company

_____
_____
_____
_____
_____

Ex. 1.6   Briefly explain the unlimited liability principle in relation to the following.

_____
_____
_____
_____
_____

Ex. 1.7   Briefly explain responsibility for debts of a company limited by shares.

_____
_____
_____
_____

Ex. 1.8   Define the following terms:
(a) Business operating cycle

_____
_____

(b) Transaction

_____

Ex. 1.9   Parties who would be interested in the financial affairs of the business.

1 The owner or manager

2 Suppliers of finance

3 Statutory authorities

Ex. 1.10   Solution in textbook.

(a) Basic accounting framework

(b) Accounting convention

(c) Accounting doctrine

(d) Historical cost accounting

Ex. 1.11   Relevant accounting convention or doctrine.

(a)

(b)

(c)

(d)

(e)

(f)

(g)

(h)

Ex. 1.12   Briefly outline the nature and purpose of accounting standards.

Ex. 1.13   Discuss how every entity is a separate accounting and a separate legal entity.

Ex. 1.14   What is a reporting entity? Discuss.

_____

_____

_____

Ex. 1.15   What is a statement of financial position? Explain.

_____

Ex. 1.16   Does the statement show the realisable value of a business? Explain.

_____

_____

Ex. 1.17   Explain the treatment of personal assets and liabilities of the proprietor.

_____

_____

Ex. 1.18   Explain the following terms:

(a) Asset _____

_____

_____

(b) Equity _____

(c) Liability _____

_____

(d) Owner's equity _____

_____

(e) Debtors _____

_____

(f) Creditors _____

_____

(g) Capital _____

_____

Ex. 1.19   Assets, liabilities or owner's equity.

(a) _____

(b) _____

(c) _____

(d) _____

(e) _____

(f) _____

(g) _____

(h) _____

(i) _____

(j) _____

(k) _____

Ex. 1.20   **Assets, liabilities or owner's equity.**

(a) _____

(b) _____

(c) _____

(d) _____

(e) _____

(f) _____

(g) _____

(h) _____

(i) _____

Ex. 1.21   **Assets, liabilities or owner's equity.**

(a) _____

(b) _____

(c) _____

(d) _____

(e) _____

(f) _____

(g) _____

(h) _____

(i) _____

(j) _____

Ex. 1.22   **Distinguish between the following terms:**

(a) **Assets** _____

     Liabilities _____

(b) **Debtors** _____

_____

     Creditors _____

_____

(c) **Cash at bank** _____

     Bank overdraft _____

_____

(d) **Loan to V Lawson** _____

     Loan from AV Finances _____

(e) **Cash on hand** _____

     Cash at bank _____

Ex. 1.23   G Rater, Retailer.

(a) Owner's equity =

(b) Statement of financial position

G Rater, Retailer
Statement of Financial Position as at 30 June 2017

Ex. 1.24   Solution in Textbook

(a) Owner's equity =

(b) Statement of financial position

Glenwood Private Hospital
Statement of Financial Position as at 30 June 2016

Ex. 1.25   E Field's Used Car Yard

(a) Owner's equity =

(b) Statement of financial position

E Field's Used Car Yard
Statement of Financial Position as at 30 June 2018

Ex. 1.26   Jakes Jeans (proprietor, C Constantinou)
(a) Owners equity =
(b) Statement of financial position

Jakes Jeans (Proprietor, C Constantinou)
Statement of Financial Position as at 30 June 2016

Ex. 1.27   Solution in textbook.
(a) Transaction analysis chart

M Travelli – Painter and Decorator
Transaction Analysis Chart

Date	Items (accounts) affected	A, L, or OE	Increase or decrease	Amount $	Explanation

(b) Statement of financial position

M Travelli – Painter and Decorator
Statement of Financial Position as at 30 June 2017

Ex. 1.28

D Fraser, Pool Supplies
Statement of Financial Position as at 31 August 2016

Ex. 1.29

Bulls Scooba Shop (proprietor D Bull)
Statement of Financial Position as at 31 May 2018

Ex. 1.30   Solution in textbook.

R Hidaka, Retailer
Statement of Financial Position as at 16 July 2017

Ex. 1.31   What is the purpose of a statement of comprehensive income?

Ex. 1.32   Income and expense transactions as distinct from a statement of financial position transaction.

Ex. 1.33   Define the following terms:

Income
_____

_____

Expense
_____

_____

Profit
_____

Loss
_____

Drawings
_____

On credit
_____

The trading process
_____

_____

Ex. 1.34   Connection between statement of comprehensive income and statement of financial position.

_____

_____

_____

Ex. 1.35   Income or expenses

(a) _____

(b) _____

(c) _____

(d) _____

(e) _____

(f) _____

(g) _____

(h) _____

(i) _____

(j) _____

(k) _____

(l) _____

Ex. 1.36 & 1.37   Assets, liabilities, owner's equity, income or expenses

1.36	1.37
(a)	(a)
(b)	(b)
(c)	(c)
(d)	(d)
(e)	(e)
(f)	(f)
(g)	(g)
(h)	(h)
(i)	(i)
(j)	(j)
(k)	(k)
(l)	(l)
(m)	(m)
(n)	(n)
(o)	(o)
(p)	(p)
(q)	(q)
(r)	(r)
(s)	(s)
(t)	(t)
(u)	(u)
(v)	(v)
(w)	(w)
(x)	(x)
	(y)
	(z)

Ex. 1.38   Assets, liabilities, Owner's equity, income or expenses

(a)	(n)
(b)	(o)
(c)	(p)
(d)	(q)
(e)	(r)
(f)	(s)
(g)	(t)
(h)	(u)
(i)	(v)
(j)	(w)
(k)	(x)
(l)	(y)
(m)	(z)

Ex. 1.39

G Glove, Gardener
Statement of comprehensive income for the year ended 30 June 2017

	$	$

Ex. 1.40

P Ricey, Retailer
Statement of comprehensive income for the year ended 30 June 2017

	$	$

Ex. 1.41

B Ryan, Retailer
Statement of comprehensive income for the year ended 31 December 2016

	$	$

Ex. 1.42

P Mason, Lawyer
Statement of comprehensive income for the year ended 30 June 2017

	$	$

Ex. 1.43

Pizza Land
Transaction Analysis Chart

Date	Items (accounts) affected	A, L, OE, I or E	Increase or decrease	Amount $

Ex. 1.44 (a)

Piper Instrument Sales
Transaction Analysis Chart

Date	Items (accounts) affected	A, L, OE, I or E	Increase or decrease	Amount $

Ex. 1.44 (b) & (c)

Piper Instrument Sales
Statement of comprehensive income for the period ending 9 October 2018

	$	$

Piper Instrument Sales
Statement of Financial Position as at 9 October 2018

Ex. 1.45 (a) & (b)

Barrassi's Butcher Shop
Statement of comprehensive income for August 2017

	$	$

Barrassi's Butcher Shop
Statement of Financial Position as at 31 August 2017

Ex. 1.46 (a) & (b)

V Lucid, Freelance Sports Writer
Statement of comprehensive income for the six months ended 30 June 2016

	$	$

V Lucid, Freelance Sports Writer
Statement of Financial Position as at 30 June 2016

Ex. 1.47 (a) & (b)   Solution in textbook.

L Vixen, Carrier
Statement of Comprehensive Income for the month ended 30 June 2017

	$	$

L Vixen, Carrier
Statement of Financial Position as at 30 June 2017

Ex. 1.48   What is a ledger account?

_____

_____

Ex. 1.49   For each of the following answer true or false:

(a) _____

(b) _____

(c) _____

(d) _____

(e) _____

(f) _____

Ex. 1.50   Outline the difference between a 'T' account and a columnar account.

 'T' account

_____

_____

 Columnar account

_____

_____

Ex. 1.51   **Fiona Shepherd, Cleaning Contractor**
                                Transaction Analysis Chart

Date	Items (accounts) affected	A, L, OE, I or E	Increase or decrease	Amount $	Debit or credit

Ex. 1.52

C Capelli, Motor Vehicle Retailer
Transaction Analysis Chart

Date	Items (accounts) affected	A, L, OE, I or E	Increase or decrease	Amount $	Debit or credit

Ex. 1.53

Geraldton Travel Service
Transaction Analysis Chart

Date	Items (accounts) affected	A, L, OE, I or E	Increase or decrease	Amount $	Debit or credit

Ex. 1.54

As Good As Mum's Laundry Service
Transaction Analysis Chart

Date	Items (accounts) affected	A, L, OE, I or E	Increase or decrease	Amount $	Debit or credit

Ex. 1.55

Green's Fashions
General Ledger
Cash at Bank Account (Asset)

Date	Particulars	Amount $	Date	Particulars	Amount $

Capital – K Green Account (Owner's equity)

Date	Particulars	Amount $	Date	Particulars	Amount $

Purchases Account (Expense)

Date	Particulars	Amount $	Date	Particulars	Amount $

Creditor – Fancy Dress Clothes Account (Liability)

Date	Particulars	Amount $	Date	Particulars	Amount $

Drawings Account (Owner's equity)

Date	Particulars	Amount $	Date	Particulars	Amount $

Sales Account (Income)

Date	Particulars	Amount $	Date	Particulars	Amount $

Debtor – B Max Account (Asset)

Date	Particulars	Amount $	Date	Particulars	Amount $

Rent Account (Expense)

Date	Particulars	Amount $	Date	Particulars	Amount $

Ex. 1.56

C Talimandis, Theatre Restaurant
General Ledger
Cash at Bank Account (Asset)

Date	Particulars	Amount $	Date	Particulars	Amount $

Capital – C Talimandis Account (Owner's equity)

Date	Particulars	Amount $	Date	Particulars	Amount $

Premises Account (Asset)

Date	Particulars	Amount $	Date	Particulars	Amount $

Equipment Account (Asset)

Date	Particulars	Amount $	Date	Particulars	Amount $

Creditor – Movie Co Account (Liability)

Date	Particulars	Amount $	Date	Particulars	Amount $

Advertising Account (Expense)

Date	Particulars	Amount $	Date	Particulars	Amount $

Fees (Takings) Account (Income)

Date	Particulars	Amount $	Date	Particulars	Amount $

Wages Account (Expense)

Date	Particulars	Amount $	Date	Particulars	Amount $

Bank Charges Account (Expense)

Date	Particulars	Amount $	Date	Particulars	Amount $

Ex. 1.57 Identify the transaction.

(a) _____

(b) _____

(c) _____

(d) _____

(e) _____

(f) _____

(g) _____

Ex. 1.58

D Cameron
General Ledger
Cash at Bank Account (Asset)

Date	Particulars	Amount $	Date	Particulars	Amount $

Furniture Account (Asset)

Date	Particulars	Amount $	Date	Particulars	Amount $

Delivery Vehicle Account (Asset)

Date	Particulars	Amount $	Date	Particulars	Amount $

Loan from E Halt Account (Liability)

Date	Particulars	Amount $	Date	Particulars	Amount $

Capital – D Cameron Account (Owner's equity)

Date	Particulars	Amount $	Date	Particulars	Amount $

Ex. 1.59

B Spender
General Ledger
Bank Overdraft Account (Liability)

Date	Particulars	Amount $	Date	Particulars	Amount $

Debtor – G Jolly Account (Asset)

Date	Particulars	Amount $	Date	Particulars	Amount $

Loan from AD Finance Account (Liability)

Date	Particulars	Amount $	Date	Particulars	Amount $

Creditor – S Haws Account (Liability)

Date	Particulars	Amount $	Date	Particulars	Amount $

Motor Vehicle Account (Asset)

Date	Particulars	Amount $	Date	Particulars	Amount $

Land and Buildings Account (Asset)

Date	Particulars	Amount $	Date	Particulars	Amount $

Capital – B Spender Account (Owner's equity)

Date	Particulars	Amount $	Date	Particulars	Amount $

Ex. 1.60

General Ledger
Cash at Bank Account

Date	Particulars	Amount $	Date	Particulars	Amount $

Fees Income Account

Date	Particulars	Amount $	Date	Particulars	Amount $

Ex. 1.61

G Elliott, Tyre Retailer
General Ledger
Cash at Bank Account (Asset)

Date	Particulars	Debit $	Credit $	Balance $

Capital – G Elliot Account (Owner's equity)

Date	Particulars	Debit $	Credit $	Balance $

Premises Account (Asset)

Date	Particulars	Debit $	Credit $	Balance $

Mortgage Loan Account (Liability)

Date	Particulars	Debit $	Credit $	Balance $

Purchases Account (Expense)

Date	Particulars	Debit $	Credit $	Balance $

Equipment Account (Asset)

Date	Particulars	Debit $	Credit $	Balance $

Creditor – Lever Co Account (Liability)

Date	Particulars	Debit $	Credit $	Balance $

Ex. 1.61

G Elliott, Tyre Retailer
General Ledger
Sales Account (Income)

Date	Particulars	Debit $	Credit $	Balance $

Debtor – R Tube Account (Asset)

Date	Particulars	Debit $	Credit $	Balance $

Wages Account (Expense)

Date	Particulars	Debit $	Credit $	Balance $

Drawings – G Elliott Account (Owner's equity)

Date	Particulars	Debit $	Credit $	Balance $

Ex. 1.62

G Lorry, Cartage Contractor
General Ledger
Cash at Bank Account (Asset)

Date	Particulars	Debit $	Credit $	Balance $

Truck Account (Asset)

Date	Particulars	Debit $	Credit $	Balance $

Equipment Account (Asset)

Date	Particulars	Debit $	Credit $	Balance $

Loan from JK Loans Account (Liability)

Date	Particulars	Debit $	Credit $	Balance $

Premises Account (Asset)

Date	Particulars	Debit $	Credit $	Balance $

Capital – G Lorry Account (Owner's equity)

Date	Particulars	Debit $	Credit $	Balance $

Fees Account (Income)

Date	Particulars	Debit $	Credit $	Balance $

Ex. 1.62   **G Lorry, Cartage Contractor**
General Ledger
Debtor – I Johns Account (Asset)

Date	Particulars	Debit $	Credit $	Balance $

Advertising Account (Expense)

Date	Particulars	Debit $	Credit $	Balance $

Electricity Account (Expense)

Date	Particulars	Debit $	Credit $	Balance $

Telephone Account (Expense)

Date	Particulars	Debit $	Credit $	Balance $

Debtor – E Ham Account (Asset)

Date	Particulars	Debit $	Credit $	Balance $

Wages Account (Expense)

Date	Particulars	Debit $	Credit $	Balance $

Computer Account (Asset)

Date	Particulars	Debit $	Credit $	Balance $

Creditor – Arco Ltd Account (Liability)

Date	Particulars	Debit $	Credit $	Balance $

Ex. 1.63

G Elliott, Tyre Retailer
Trial Balance as at 30 April 2019

Account name	Debit $	Credit $

Ex. 1.64

G Lorry, Cartage Contractor
Trial Balance as at 31 July 2017

Account name	Debit $	Credit $

Ex. 1.65   Explain 'trial balance'.

_____
_____
_____
_____

Ex. 1.66   Explain at least three limitations of a trial balance.

_____
_____
_____
_____
_____
_____
_____
_____
_____
_____

Ex. 1.67 (a) Solution in textbook.

Cristodulou Floor Coverings
General Ledger
Cash at Bank Account (Asset)

Date	Particulars	Amount $	Date	Particulars	Amount $

Shop Premises Account (Asset)

Date	Particulars	Amount $	Date	Particulars	Amount $

Trading Stock Account (Asset)

Date	Particulars	Amount $	Date	Particulars	Amount $

Motor Vehicle Account (Asset)

Date	Particulars	Amount $	Date	Particulars	Amount $

Ex. 1.67 (a) Solution in textbook.

Cristodulou Floor Coverings
General Ledger
Creditor – D Frost Account (Liability)

Date	Particulars	Amount $	Date	Particulars	Amount $

Furniture and Fittings Account (Asset)

Date	Particulars	Amount $	Date	Particulars	Amount $

Debtor – S Hall Account (Asset)

Date	Particulars	Amount $	Date	Particulars	Amount $

Capital – A Cristodulou Account (Owner's equity)

Date	Particulars	Amount $	Date	Particulars	Amount $

Purchases Account (Expense)

Date	Particulars	Amount $	Date	Particulars	Amount $

Loan from Berber Finance Co Account (Liability)

Date	Particulars	Amount $	Date	Particulars	Amount $

Sales Account (Income)

Date	Particulars	Amount $	Date	Particulars	Amount $

Ex. 1.67 (a) Solution in textbook.

Cristodulou Floor Coverings
General Ledger
Wages Account (Expense)

Date	Particulars	Amount $	Date	Particulars	Amount $

Power and Light Account (Expense)

Date	Particulars	Amount $	Date	Particulars	Amount $

Cleaning Account (Expense)

Date	Particulars	Amount $	Date	Particulars	Amount $

Drawings – A Cristodulou Account (Owner's equity)

Date	Particulars	Amount $	Date	Particulars	Amount $

Ex. 1.67 (b)

Cristodulou Floor Coverings
Trial Balance as at 31 January 2017

Account name	Debit $	Credit $

Ex. 1.68 (a)

P Hammer
General Ledger
Cash at Bank Account (Asset)

Date	Particulars	Amount $		Date	Particulars	Amount $

Capital – P Hammer Account (Owner's equity)

Date	Particulars	Amount $		Date	Particulars	Amount $

Truck Account (Asset)

Date	Particulars	Amount $		Date	Particulars	Amount $

Drilling Auger Account (Asset)

Date	Particulars	Amount $		Date	Particulars	Amount $

Trailer Account (Asset)

Date	Particulars	Amount $		Date	Particulars	Amount $

Fees Account (Income)

Date	Particulars	Amount $		Date	Particulars	Amount $

Petrol and Oil Account (Expense)

Date	Particulars	Amount $		Date	Particulars	Amount $

Ex. 1.68 (a)

P Hammer
General Ledger
Equipment Repairs Account (Expense)

Date	Particulars	Amount $	Date	Particulars	Amount $

Advertising Account (Expense)

Date	Particulars	Amount $	Date	Particulars	Amount $

Debtor – S Trainer Account (Asset)

Date	Particulars	Amount $	Date	Particulars	Amount $

Drawings Account – P Hammer (Owner's equity)

Date	Particulars	Amount $	Date	Particulars	Amount $

Casual Wages Account (Expense)

Date	Particulars	Amount $	Date	Particulars	Amount $

Ex. 1.68 (b)

P Hammer
Trial Balance as at 12 March 2016

Account name	Debit $	Credit $

Ex. 1.69 (a)

Big Book Sales
General Ledger
Cash at Bank Account (Asset)

Date	Particulars	Debit $	Credit $	Balance $

Stock Account (Asset)

Date	Particulars	Debit $	Credit $	Balance $

Furniture and Fittings Account (Asset)

Date	Particulars	Debit $	Credit $	Balance $

Capital – B Rowe Account (Owner's equity)

Date	Particulars	Debit $	Credit $	Balance $

Purchases Account (Expense)

Date	Particulars	Debit $	Credit $	Balance $

Creditor – Worm Industries Account (Liability)

Date	Particulars	Debit $	Credit $	Balance $

Sales Account (Income)

Date	Particulars	Debit $	Credit $	Balance $

Ex. 1.69 (a)

Big Book Sales
General Ledger
Debtor – N Cooke Account (Asset)

Date	Particulars	Debit $	Credit $	Balance $

Rent Account (Expense)

Date	Particulars	Debit $	Credit $	Balance $

Wages Account (Expense)

Date	Particulars	Debit $	Credit $	Balance $

Creditor – AL Design Account (Liability)

Date	Particulars	Debit $	Credit $	Balance $

Ex. 1.69 (b)

Big Book Sales
Trial Balance as at 30 June 2017

Account name	Debit $	Credit $

Ex. 1.70 (a)

Cooke's Auto Service
General Ledger
Bank Overdraft Account (Liability)

Date	Particulars	Debit $	Credit $	Balance $

Land and Buildings Account (Asset)

Date	Particulars	Debit $	Credit $	Balance $

Debtor – G Osborne Account (Asset)

Date	Particulars	Debit $	Credit $	Balance $

Creditor – I Castles Account (Liability)

Date	Particulars	Debit $	Credit $	Balance $

Motor Vehicles Account (Asset)

Date	Particulars	Debit $	Credit $	Balance $

Mortgage on Land and Buildings Account (Liability)

Date	Particulars	Debit $	Credit $	Balance $

Ex. 1.70 (a)

Cooke's Auto Service
General Ledger
Furniture and Equipment Account (Asset)

Date	Particulars	Debit $	Credit $	Balance $

Capital – Z Cooke Account (Owner's equity)

Date	Particulars	Debit $	Credit $	Balance $

Fees Account (Income)

Date	Particulars	Debit $	Credit $	Balance $

Rates Account (Expense)

Date	Particulars	Debit $	Credit $	Balance $

Vehicle Parts Account (Expense)

Date	Particulars	Debit $	Credit $	Balance $

Mechanics' Wages Account (Expense)

Date	Particulars	Debit $	Credit $	Balance $

Debtor – Dee Transport Co Account (Asset)

Date	Particulars	Debit $	Credit $	Balance $

Ex. 1.70 (a)

Cooke's Auto Service
General Ledger
Mortgage Interest Account (Expense)

Date	Particulars	Debit $	Credit $	Balance $

Bank Interest Account (Expense)

Date	Particulars	Debit $	Credit $	Balance $

Accounting Fees Account (Expense)

Date	Particulars	Debit $	Credit $	Balance $

Ex. 1.70 (b)

Cooke's Auto Service
Trial Balance as at 31 August 2017

Account name	Debit $	Credit $

Ex. 1.71   Discuss how the General Ledger is supported by other ledgers.

_____

_____

_____

_____

_____

_____

_____

_____

_____

Ex. 1.72   Discuss the advantages of subsidiary ledgers in an accounting system.

_____

_____

_____

_____

_____

_____

_____

_____

_____

_____

_____

Ex. 1.73 (a)

Grass's Mowing Service
General Ledger
Cash at Bank Account (Asset)

Date	Particulars	Debit $	Credit $	Balance $

Capital – L Grass Account (Owner's equity)

Date	Particulars	Debit $	Credit $	Balance $

Ex. 1.73 (a)

Grass's Mowing Service
General Ledger
Mowers Account (Asset)

Date	Particulars	Debit $	Credit $	Balance $

Motor Vehicle Account (Asset)

Date	Particulars	Debit $	Credit $	Balance $

Creditor – TY Motors Account (Liability)

Date	Particulars	Debit $	Credit $	Balance $

Petrol and Oil Account (Expense)

Date	Particulars	Debit $	Credit $	Balance $

Creditor – Fred's Garage Account (Liability)

Date	Particulars	Debit $	Credit $	Balance $

Trailer Account (Asset)

Date	Particulars	Debit $	Credit $	Balance $

Advertising Account (Expense)

Date	Particulars	Debit $	Credit $	Balance $

Ex. 1.73 (a)

Grass's Mowing Service
General Ledger
Fees Account (Income)

Date	Particulars	Debit $	Credit $	Balance $

Drawings – L Grass Account (Owner's equity)

Date	Particulars	Debit $	Credit $	Balance $

Tools Account (Asset)

Date	Particulars	Debit $	Credit $	Balance $

Debtor – I Couch Account (Asset)

Date	Particulars	Debit $	Credit $	Balance $

Repairs Account (Expense)

Date	Particulars	Debit $	Credit $	Balance $

Wages Account (Expense)

Date	Particulars	Debit $	Credit $	Balance $

Ex. 1.73 (b)

Grass's Mowing Service
Trial Balance as at 14 October 2018

Account name	Debit $	Credit $

Ex. 1.74 (a)   Solution in textbook.

Big Cat Studio
General Ledger
Cash at Bank Account (Asset)

Date	Particulars	Debit $	Credit $	Balance $

Motor Vehicles Account (Asset)

Date	Particulars	Debit $	Credit $	Balance $

Capital – S Panda Account (Owner's Equity)

Date	Particulars	Debit $	Credit $	Balance $

Premises Account (Asset)

Date	Particulars	Debit $	Credit $	Balance $

Mortgage Loan on Premises Account (Liability)

Date	Particulars	Debit $	Credit $	Balance $

Ex. 1.74 (a)   Solution in textbook.

Big Cat Studio
General Ledger
Fixtures and Fittings Account (Asset)

Date	Particulars	Debit $	Credit $	Balance $

Equipment Account (Asset)

Date	Particulars	Debit $	Credit $	Balance $

Computer Account (Asset)

Date	Particulars	Debit $	Credit $	Balance $

Creditor – Myroc Computers Account (Liability)

Date	Particulars	Debit $	Credit $	Balance $

Fees Account (Income)

Date	Particulars	Debit $	Credit $	Balance $

Electricity Account (Expense)

Date	Particulars	Debit $	Credit $	Balance $

Commission Account (Expense)

Date	Particulars	Debit $	Credit $	Balance $

Ex. 1.74 (a)   Solution in textbook.

Big Cat Studio
General Ledger
Debtor – W Hip Account (Asset)

Date	Particulars	Debit $	Credit $	Balance $

Debtor – F Lash Account (Asset)

Date	Particulars	Debit $	Credit $	Balance $

Advertising Account (Expense)

Date	Particulars	Debit $	Credit $	Balance $

Office Wages Account (Expense)

Date	Particulars	Debit $	Credit $	Balance $

Rates Account (Expense)

Date	Particulars	Debit $	Credit $	Balance $

Drawings – S Panda Account (Owner's Equity)

Date	Particulars	Debit $	Credit $	Balance $

Laundering Account (Expense)

Date	Particulars	Debit $	Credit $	Balance $

Ex. 1.74 (b)   Solution in textbook.

Big Cat Studio
Trial Balance as at 30 November 2017

Account name	Debit $	Credit $

Ex. 1.75 (a)

Bloom's Florist Shop
General Ledger
Cash at Bank Account (Asset)

Date	Particulars	Debit $	Credit $	Balance $

Debtor – A Pansy Account (Asset)

Date	Particulars	Debit $	Credit $	Balance $

Creditor – P Ivy Account (Liability)

Date	Particulars	Debit $	Credit $	Balance $

Stock Account (Asset)

Date	Particulars	Debit $	Credit $	Balance $

Mortgage Loan Account (Liability)

Date	Particulars	Debit $	Credit $	Balance $

Premises Account (Asset)

Date	Particulars	Debit $	Credit $	Balance $

Ex. 1.75 (a)

Bloom's Florist Shop
General Ledger
Shop Fittings Account (Asset)

Date	Particulars	Debit $	Credit $	Balance $

Equipment Account (Asset)

Date	Particulars	Debit $	Credit $	Balance $

Capital – G Bloom Account (Owner's equity)

Date	Particulars	Debit $	Credit $	Balance $

Sales Account (Income)

Date	Particulars	Debit $	Credit $	Balance $

Purchases Account (Expense)

Date	Particulars	Debit $	Credit $	Balance $

Creditor – Flowerquip Co Account (Liability)

Date	Particulars	Debit $	Credit $	Balance $

Drawings – G Bloom Account (Owner's equity)

Date	Particulars	Debit $	Credit $	Balance $

Commission Income Account (Income)

Date	Particulars	Debit $	Credit $	Balance $

Casual Wages Account (Expense)

Date	Particulars	Debit $	Credit $	Balance $

Ex. 1.75 (a)

Bloom's Florist Shop
General Ledger
Interest on Mortgage Loan Account (Expense)

Date	Particulars	Debit $	Credit $	Balance $

Rates Account (Expense)

Date	Particulars	Debit $	Credit $	Balance $

Ex. 1.75 (b)

Bloom's Florist Shop
Trial Balance as at 31 July 2019

Account name	Debit $	Credit $

Ex. 1.76

T Chan, Retailer
General Ledger
Cash at Bank Account

Date	Particulars	Debit $	Credit $	Balance $

Stock Account

Date	Particulars	Debit $	Credit $	Balance $

Capital – C Chan Account

Date	Particulars	Debit $	Credit $	Balance $

Purchases Account

Date	Particulars	Debit $	Credit $	Balance $

Ex. 1.77

S Dixon, Retailer
General Ledger
Cash at Bank Account

Date	Particulars	Debit $	Credit $	Balance $

Loan from Better Financing Account

Date	Particulars	Debit $	Credit $	Balance $

Stock Account

Date	Particulars	Debit $	Credit $	Balance $

Land and Buildings Account

Date	Particulars	Debit $	Credit $	Balance $

Capital – S Dixon Account

Date	Particulars	Debit $	Credit $	Balance $

Purchases Account

Date	Particulars	Debit $	Credit $	Balance $

Creditor – BY Supplies Account

Date	Particulars	Debit $	Credit $	Balance $

Ex. 1.78

B Browning, Retailer
General Ledger
Purchases Account

Date	Particulars	Debit $	Credit $	Balance $

Cash at Bank Account

Date	Particulars	Debit $	Credit $	Balance $

Creditor – Murray Manufacturing Account

Date	Particulars	Debit $	Credit $	Balance $

Purchases Returns and Allowances Account

Date	Particulars	Debit $	Credit $	Balance $

Ex. 1.79

B Arthur, Retailer
General Ledger
Purchases Account

Date	Particulars	Debit $	Credit $	Balance $

Creditor – Mini Wholesalers Account

Date	Particulars	Debit $	Credit $	Balance $

Purchase Returns and Allowances Account

Date	Particulars	Debit $	Credit $	Balance $

Cash at Bank Account

Date	Particulars	Debit $	Credit $	Balance $

Ex. 1.80

A Grant, Shopkeeper
General Ledger
Cash at Bank Account

Date	Particulars	Debit $	Credit $	Balance $

Sales Account

Date	Particulars	Debit $	Credit $	Balance $

Debtor – M Ajor Account

Date	Particulars	Debit $	Credit $	Balance $

Ex. 1.81

S Short, Retailer
General Ledger
Cash at Bank Account

Date	Particulars	Debit $	Credit $	Balance $

Sales Account

Date	Particulars	Debit $	Credit $	Balance $

Debtor – G Georgiou Account

Date	Particulars	Debit $	Credit $	Balance $

Ex. 1.82

P Clements, Merchant
General Ledger
Cash at Bank Account

Date	Particulars	Debit $	Credit $	Balance $

Sales Account

Date	Particulars	Debit $	Credit $	Balance $

Debtor – T Nelson Account

Date	Particulars	Debit $	Credit $	Balance $

Sales Returns and Allowances Account

Date	Particulars	Debit $	Credit $	Balance $

Ex. 1.83   **M Tan, Retailer**
                                      General Ledger
                                   Cash at Bank Account

Date	Particulars	Debit $	Credit $	Balance $

Sales Account

Date	Particulars	Debit $	Credit $	Balance $

Debtor – D Parsons Account

Date	Particulars	Debit $	Credit $	Balance $

Sales Returns and Allowances Account

Date	Particulars	Debit $	Credit $	Balance $

Ex. 1.84 (a)

S Vella, Retailer
General Ledger
Cash at Bank Account

Date	Particulars	Debit $	Credit $	Balance $

Stock Account

Date	Particulars	Debit $	Credit $	Balance $

Premises Account

Date	Particulars	Debit $	Credit $	Balance $

Furniture Account

Date	Particulars	Debit $	Credit $	Balance $

Capital – S Vella Account

Date	Particulars	Debit $	Credit $	Balance $

Purchases Account

Date	Particulars	Debit $	Credit $	Balance $

Sales Account

Date	Particulars	Debit $	Credit $	Balance $

Ex. 1.84 (a)

S Vella, Retailer
General Ledger
Debtor – J Osborne Account

Date	Particulars	Debit $	Credit $	Balance $

Creditor – J Bramley Account

Date	Particulars	Debit $	Credit $	Balance $

Sales Returns and Allowances Account

Date	Particulars	Debit $	Credit $	Balance $

Purchases Returns and Allowances Account

Date	Particulars	Debit $	Credit $	Balance $

Ex. 1.84

S Vella, Retailer
Trial Balance as at 31 July 2017

Account name	Debit $	Credit $

Ex. 1.85 (a)

B Gunge, Retailer
General Ledger
Cash at Bank Account

Date	Particulars	Debit $	Credit $	Balance $

Stock Account

Date	Particulars	Debit $	Credit $	Balance $

Motor Vehicle Account

Date	Particulars	Debit $	Credit $	Balance $

Loan from AZ Bank Ltd Account

Date	Particulars	Debit $	Credit $	Balance $

Capital – B Gunge Account

Date	Particulars	Debit $	Credit $	Balance $

Purchases Account

Date	Particulars	Debit $	Credit $	Balance $

Creditor – AG Supplies Account

Date	Particulars	Debit $	Credit $	Balance $

Ex. 1.85 (a)

B Gunge, Retailer
General Ledger
Sales Account

Date	Particulars	Debit $	Credit $	Balance $

Purchases Returns and Allowances Account

Date	Particulars	Debit $	Credit $	Balance $

Debtor – P Love Account

Date	Particulars	Debit $	Credit $	Balance $

Sales Returns and Allowances Account

Date	Particulars	Debit $	Credit $	Balance $

Ex. 1.85 (b)

B Gunge, Retailer
Trial Balance as at 11 August 2017

Account name	Debit $	Credit $

Ex. 1.86

J Brown, Grocer
General Ledger
Drawings – J Brown Account

Date	Particulars	Debit $	Credit $	Balance $

Purchases Account

Date	Particulars	Debit $	Credit $	Balance $

Cash at Bank Account

Date	Particulars	Debit $	Credit $	Balance $

Ex. 1.87

D Ogg, Pet Shop Owner
General Ledger
Cash at Bank Account

Date	Particulars	Debit $	Credit $	Balance $

Stock Account

Date	Particulars	Debit $	Credit $	Balance $

Capital – D Ogg Account

Date	Particulars	Debit $	Credit $	Balance $

Purchases Account

Date	Particulars	Debit $	Credit $	Balance $

Creditor – Pet Supplies Account

Date	Particulars	Debit $	Credit $	Balance $

Drawings – D Ogg Account

Date	Particulars	Debit $	Credit $	Balance $

Ex. 1.88

A Mahfouz
General Ledger
Debtor – P Lazenby Account

Date	Particulars	Debit $	Credit $	Balance $

Sales Account

Date	Particulars	Debit $	Credit $	Balance $

Cash at Bank Account

Date	Particulars	Debit $	Credit $	Balance $

Sales Returns and Allowances Account

Date	Particulars	Debit $	Credit $	Balance $

Discount Expense Account

Date	Particulars	Debit $	Credit $	Balance $

Ex. 1.89   **G Wills, Soft-drink Stall**
                                        General Ledger
                                        Stock Account

Date	Particulars	Debit $	Credit $	Balance $

Cash at Bank Account

Date	Particulars	Debit $	Credit $	Balance $

Capital – G Wills Account

Date	Particulars	Debit $	Credit $	Balance $

Purchases Account

Date	Particulars	Debit $	Credit $	Balance $

Creditor – Harry's Drinks Account

Date	Particulars	Debit $	Credit $	Balance $

Purchases Returns and Allowances Account

Date	Particulars	Debit $	Credit $	Balance $

Discount Income Account

Date	Particulars	Debit $	Credit $	Balance $

Ex. 1.90

N Taylor, Retailer
General Ledger
Debtor – H Peters Account

Date	Particulars	Debit $	Credit $	Balance $

Creditor – J Downing

Date	Particulars	Debit $	Credit $	Balance $

Ex. 1.91

O North, Importer
General Ledger
Debtor – I Skint Account

Date	Particulars	Debit $	Credit $	Balance $

Sales Account

Date	Particulars	Debit $	Credit $	Balance $

Late Fees Income Account

Date	Particulars	Debit $	Credit $	Balance $

Bad Debts Account

Date	Particulars	Debit $	Credit $	Balance $

Ex. 1.92

G Big, Retailer
General Ledger
Debtor – B Purt Account

Date	Particulars	Debit $	Credit $	Balance $

Sales Account

Date	Particulars	Debit $	Credit $	Balance $

Sales Returns and Allowances Account

Date	Particulars	Debit $	Credit $	Balance $

Cash at Bank Account

Date	Particulars	Debit $	Credit $	Balance $

Bad Debts Account

Date	Particulars	Debit $	Credit $	Balance $

Ex. 1.93

Melon the Greengrocer
General Ledger
Capital – J Melon Account

Date	Particulars	Debit $	Credit $	Balance $

Cash at Bank Account

Date	Particulars	Debit $	Credit $	Balance $

Mortgage Loan Account

Date	Particulars	Debit $	Credit $	Balance $

Power and Light Account

Date	Particulars	Debit $	Credit $	Balance $

Land and Buildings Account

Date	Particulars	Debit $	Credit $	Balance $

Purchases Account

Date	Particulars	Debit $	Credit $	Balance $

Ex. 1.93

Melon the Greengrocer
General Ledger
Stock Account

Date	Particulars	Debit $	Credit $	Balance $

Fittings and Equipment Account

Date	Particulars	Debit $	Credit $	Balance $

Sales Account

Date	Particulars	Debit $	Credit $	Balance $

Debtor – R Brown Account

Date	Particulars	Debit $	Credit $	Balance $

Creditor – M Meyer Account

Date	Particulars	Debit $	Credit $	Balance $

Wages Account

Date	Particulars	Debit $	Credit $	Balance $

Debtor – J Atkins Account

Date	Particulars	Debit $	Credit $	Balance $

Sales Returns and Allowances Account

Date	Particulars	Debit $	Credit $	Balance $

Ex. 1.93

Melon the Greengrocer
General Ledger
Discount Expense Account

Date	Particulars	Debit $	Credit $	Balance $

Discount Income Account

Date	Particulars	Debit $	Credit $	Balance $

Purchases Returns and Allowances Account

Date	Particulars	Debit $	Credit $	Balance $

Interest Expense Account

Date	Particulars	Debit $	Credit $	Balance $

Melon the Greengrocer
Trial Balance as at 31 March 2018

Account name	Debit $	Credit $

Ex. 1.94　　　**True or false.**

(a) _____

(b) _____

(c) _____

(d) _____

(e) _____

(f) _____

(g) _____

Ex. 1.95

C McReilly
General Ledger
Cash at Bank Account

Date	Particulars	Debit $	Credit $	Balance $

Stock Account

Date	Particulars	Debit $	Credit $	Balance $

Building Account

Date	Particulars	Debit $	Credit $	Balance $

Fixtures Account

Date	Particulars	Debit $	Credit $	Balance $

Ex. 1.95

C McReilly
General Ledger
Mortgage Loan on Buildings Account

Date	Particulars	Debit $	Credit $	Balance $

Capital – C McReilly Account

Date	Particulars	Debit $	Credit $	Balance $

Purchases Account

Date	Particulars	Debit $	Credit $	Balance $

Creditor – A Wily Account

Date	Particulars	Debit $	Credit $	Balance $

Purchase Returns and Allowances Account

Date	Particulars	Debit $	Credit $	Balance $

Motor Vehicle Account

Date	Particulars	Debit $	Credit $	Balance $

Creditor – Vroom Motors Ltd Account

Date	Particulars	Debit $	Credit $	Balance $

Discount Income Account

Date	Particulars	Debit $	Credit $	Balance $

Ex. 1.95

C McReilly
General Ledger
Sales Account

Date	Particulars	Debit $	Credit $	Balance $

Debtor – S Pooner Account

Date	Particulars	Debit $	Credit $	Balance $

Sales Returns and Allowances Account

Date	Particulars	Debit $	Credit $	Balance $

Wages Account

Date	Particulars	Debit $	Credit $	Balance $

Creditor – D Brown Account

Date	Particulars	Debit $	Credit $	Balance $

Land Account

Date	Particulars	Debit $	Credit $	Balance $

Mortgage Loan on Land Account

Date	Particulars	Debit $	Credit $	Balance $

Ex. 1.95

C McReilly
General Ledger
Discount Expense Account

Date	Particulars	Debit $	Credit $	Balance $

Drawings – C McReilly Account

Date	Particulars	Debit $	Credit $	Balance $

C McReilly
Trial Balance as at 30 September 2016

Account name	Debit $	Credit $

Ex. 1.96 Solution in textbook.

Roger's Deli
General Ledger
Cash at Bank Account

Date	Particulars	Debit $	Credit $	Balance $

Capital – R Williams Account

Date	Particulars	Debit $	Credit $	Balance $

Cash on Hand Account

Date	Particulars	Debit $	Credit $	Balance $

Delivery Vehicle Account

Date	Particulars	Debit $	Credit $	Balance $

Drawings – R Williams Account

Date	Particulars	Debit $	Credit $	Balance $

Electricity Account

Date	Particulars	Debit $	Credit $	Balance $

Ex. 1.96   Solution in textbook.

Roger's Deli
General Ledger
Furniture and Fittings Account

Date	Particulars	Debit $	Credit $	Balance $

Investments Account

Date	Particulars	Debit $	Credit $	Balance $

Loan from OP Loans Account

Date	Particulars	Debit $	Credit $	Balance $

Purchases Account

Date	Particulars	Debit $	Credit $	Balance $

Rent Account

Date	Particulars	Debit $	Credit $	Balance $

Sales Account

Date	Particulars	Debit $	Credit $	Balance $

Stock Account

Date	Particulars	Debit $	Credit $	Balance $

Ex. 1.96 Solution in textbook.

Roger's Deli
General Ledger
Debtor – S Fitt Account

Date	Particulars	Debit $	Credit $	Balance $

Creditor – B Broom Account

Date	Particulars	Debit $	Credit $	Balance $

Wages Account

Date	Particulars	Debit $	Credit $	Balance $

Creditor – Maxi Co Account

Date	Particulars	Debit $	Credit $	Balance $

Discount Expense Account

Date	Particulars	Debit $	Credit $	Balance $

Purchase Returns and Allowances Account

Date	Particulars	Debit $	Credit $	Balance $

Ex. 1.96   Solution in textbook.

Roger's Deli
General Ledger
Interest Expense Account

Date	Particulars	Debit $	Credit $	Balance $

Vehicle Repairs Account

Date	Particulars	Debit $	Credit $	Balance $

Discount Income Account

Date	Particulars	Debit $	Credit $	Balance $

Bad Debts Account

Date	Particulars	Debit $	Credit $	Balance $

Roger's Deli
Trial Balance as at 31 October 2017

Account name	Debit $	Credit $

Ex. 1.97

Pete's Service Station
General Ledger
Capital – Peter Da Silva Account

Date	Particulars	Debit $	Credit $	Balance $

Cash at Bank Account

Date	Particulars	Debit $	Credit $	Balance $

Creditor – A Ralph Account

Date	Particulars	Debit $	Credit $	Balance $

Debtor – D Ball Account

Date	Particulars	Debit $	Credit $	Balance $

Equipment Account

Date	Particulars	Debit $	Credit $	Balance $

Ex. 1.97

Pete's Service Station
General Ledger
Loan to D Dillon Account

Date	Particulars	Debit $	Credit $	Balance $

Mechanics' Wages Account

Date	Particulars	Debit $	Credit $	Balance $

Power and Light Account

Date	Particulars	Debit $	Credit $	Balance $

Premises Account

Date	Particulars	Debit $	Credit $	Balance $

Purchases – Parts Account

Date	Particulars	Debit $	Credit $	Balance $

Purchases – Petrol and Oil Account

Date	Particulars	Debit $	Credit $	Balance $

Sales – Petrol and Oil Account

Date	Particulars	Debit $	Credit $	Balance $

Stock of Parts Account

Date	Particulars	Debit $	Credit $	Balance $

Ex. 1.97

Pete's Service Station
General Ledger
Stock of Petrol and Oil Account

Date	Particulars	Debit $	Credit $	Balance $

Vehicle Servicing Fees Account

Date	Particulars	Debit $	Credit $	Balance $

Drawings – Peter Da Silva Account

Date	Particulars	Debit $	Credit $	Balance $

Creditor – Mogil Ltd Account

Date	Particulars	Debit $	Credit $	Balance $

Creditor – Rapco Account

Date	Particulars	Debit $	Credit $	Balance $

Debtor – A Benson Account

Date	Particulars	Debit $	Credit $	Balance $

Discount Expense Account

Date	Particulars	Debit $	Credit $	Balance $

Interest Income Account

Date	Particulars	Debit $	Credit $	Balance $

Discount Income Account

Date	Particulars	Debit $	Credit $	Balance $

Ex. 1.97

Pete's Service Station
General Ledger
Purchase Returns and Allowances – Parts Account

Date	Particulars	Debit $	Credit $	Balance $

Filing Cabinet Account

Date	Particulars	Debit $	Credit $	Balance $

Bad Debts Account

Date	Particulars	Debit $	Credit $	Balance $

Pete's Service Station
Trial Balance as at 31 May 2016

Account name	Debit $	Credit $

Ex. 1.98   **Y Mitropolous, Horse Trainer**
                                  Chart of accounts

Ex. 1.99   **P Tomas, Retailer**
                                  Chart of accounts

Ex. 1.100

A Fouad, Gift Shop
Chart of accounts

_____

_____

_____

_____

_____

_____

_____

_____

_____

_____

_____

_____

_____

_____

_____

_____

Ex. 1.101 (a)

Chambers Canvas and Camping Gear
General Ledger
Cash at Bank Account

Date	Particulars	Debit $	Credit $	Balance $

Furniture and Fittings Account

Date	Particulars	Debit $	Credit $	Balance $

Loan to Bruce Guyrope Account

Date	Particulars	Debit $	Credit $	Balance $

Motor Vehicles Account

Date	Particulars	Debit $	Credit $	Balance $

Land and Buildings Account

Date	Particulars	Debit $	Credit $	Balance $

Ex. 1.101 (a)

Chambers Canvas and Camping Gear
General Ledger
Accounts Payable Control Account

Date	Particulars	Debit $	Credit $	Balance $

Accounts Receivable Control Account

Date	Particulars	Debit $	Credit $	Balance $

Capital – Paul Chambers Account

Date	Particulars	Debit $	Credit $	Balance $

Drawings – Paul Chambers Account

Date	Particulars	Debit $	Credit $	Balance $

Advertising Account

Date	Particulars	Debit $	Credit $	Balance $

Discount Expense Account

Date	Particulars	Debit $	Credit $	Balance $

Ex. 1.101 (a)

Chambers Canvas and Camping Gear
General Ledger
Discount Income Account

Date	Particulars	Debit $	Credit $	Balance $

Power and Light Account

Date	Particulars	Debit $	Credit $	Balance $

Freight and Cartage Account

Date	Particulars	Debit $	Credit $	Balance $

Insurance Account

Date	Particulars	Debit $	Credit $	Balance $

Interest Income Account

Date	Particulars	Debit $	Credit $	Balance $

Motor Vehicle Running Costs Account

Date	Particulars	Debit $	Credit $	Balance $

Purchases Account

Date	Particulars	Debit $	Credit $	Balance $

Purchases Returns and Allowances Account

Date	Particulars	Debit $	Credit $	Balance $

Exercise 1.101 (a) (3)   **Page 88**

Ex. 1.101 (a)

Chambers Canvas and Camping Gear
General Ledger
Rates and Taxes Account

Date	Particulars	Debit $	Credit $	Balance $

Sales Account

Date	Particulars	Debit $	Credit $	Balance $

Sales Returns and Allowances Account

Date	Particulars	Debit $	Credit $	Balance $

Wages Account

Date	Particulars	Debit $	Credit $	Balance $

Stock on Hand Account

Date	Particulars	Debit $	Credit $	Balance $

Bad Debts Account

Date	Particulars	Debit $	Credit $	Balance $

Cleaning Account

Date	Particulars	Debit $	Credit $	Balance $

Ex. 1.101 (b)

Chambers Canvas and Camping Gear
Trial Balance as at 31 July 2017

Account name	Debit $	Credit $

Ex. 1.101 (c)

Chambers Canvas and Camping Gear
Chart of accounts

_____

_____

_____

_____

_____

_____

_____

_____

_____

_____

_____

_____

_____

_____

_____

_____

_____

_____

_____

_____

_____

_____

Ex. 1.102   Briefly outline the factors that influence the design of an accounting system.

_____

_____

_____

Ex. 2.1   Discuss the role of business documents in the accounting process.

_____

_____

_____

_____

_____

Ex. 2.2   Discuss the purpose of 'pre-numbered' business documents.

_____

_____

_____

_____

Ex. 2.3   **Documents used:**

(a) _____

(b) _____

(c) _____

(d) _____

(e) _____

(f) _____

Ex. 2.4   **Documents used:**

(a) _____

(b) _____

(c) _____

(d) _____

(e) _____

(f) _____

(g) _____

(h) _____

(i) _____

(j) _____

(k) _____

Ex. 2.5

No. 470 Date _____ To _____ For _____ (GST included $_____)	Bank of Australia Shelton Branch	No. 470 Stamp duty paid
	Pay_____ or bearer	Date _____

	Balance	The sum of	_____
	Deposits		
			$_____
	This cheque		
	Balance	_____	

Receipt   Clarry's Cartage Service

Number _____
Date   _____

Received from   _____

The sum of _____ **dollars and**

_____ **cents**

For

_____ (inc. GST $ ___)

Discount _____ (inc. GST $ ___)

Signed _____

Tax Invoice

Clarry's Cartage Service
45 Bandit Road,
Shelton 3800
ABN 45 652 111 223

Number_____
Date_____

Debit to

_____
_____
_____

Order no. ....

Description	Quantity	Unit Price (inc. GST)	Amount (inc. GST)
		$	$
GST included in this invoice $			

Ex. 2.5

Tax Invoice	Zero Oil Supplies 75 Gasoline Grove, Shelton 3800 ABN 36 547 589 223	Number _____ Date _____
Debit to		**Order no.** ....

Description	Quantity	Unit Price (inc. GST) $	Amount (inc. GST) $
GST included in this invoice $			

Adjustment Note	Clarry's Cartage Service 45 Bandit Road, Shelton 3800 ABN 45 652 111 223	Number _____ Date _____
Credit to		**Invoice no.** .... **Invoice date** ....

Description		Unit Price (inc. GST) $	Amount (inc. GST) $
	GST included in this adjustment note $		
Reasons for credit *1 hour delay*			

No. 471 Date _____ To _____ For _____ *Discount $ (inc. $ GST)*	Bank of Australia Shelton Branch	No. 471 Stamp duty paid Date _____
	Pay_____ or bearer	
_____ **Balance** _____ **Deposits** _____ _____ **This cheque** _____ **Balance**	The sum of_____ _____ $ _____	

Ex. 2.6

Tax Invoice	Bunny's Pet Shop 14 Ferret Drive, Jackson 5997 ABN 78 921 444 556	Number _____ Date _____
Debit to _____ _____ _____		Order no. ....

Description	Quantity	Unit Price (inc. GST) $	Amount (inc. GST) $
GST included in this invoice $			

No. 4761 Date _____ To _____ For _____ (GST included $)	Bank of Victoria Jackson West	No. 4761 Stamp duty paid Date 2/7/2017
☐ **Balance** ☐ **Deposits** ☐ **This cheque** ☐ **Balance**	Pay_____ or bearer The sum of _____ _____ $ _____	

Purchase order **To** _____ _____ _____	Bunny's Pet Shop 14 Ferret Drive, Jackson 5997 ABN 78 921 444 556	Number _____ Date _____

Quantity	Description	Estimated Price (inc. GST) $

Delivery by:	Method _____
	Date _____ Authorised by _____

Ex. 2.6

Delivery Docket	Number _____	Date _____

Deliver from   B Black, 15 Greystone Road,
Jackson 5997

Deliver to   _____
_____

The following goods:

Quantity	Description
- - - - - - -	- -
- - - - - - -	- -
- - - - - - -	- -

Method of delivery_____
Received in good order and condition

_____
(Signature of receiver)

Tax Invoice	B Black, 15 Greystone Road, Jackson 3997 ABN 98 777 825 369	Number _____ Date _____

Debit to
_____
_____
_____

Order no. ....

Description	Quantity	Unit Price (inc. GST) $	Amount (inc. GST) $
- - - - - - - - - - - - - - - - -	- - - - - - - - - - - - -	- - - - - - - - - - -	- - - - - - - - - - -
- - - - - - - - - - - - - - - - -	- - - - - - - - - - - - -	- - - - - - - - - - -	- - - - - - - - - - -
- - - - - - - - - - - - - - - - -	- - - - - - - - - - - - -	- - - - - - - - - - -	- - - - - - - - - - -
GST included in this invoice $_____			

Adjustment Note	Bunny's Pet Shop 14 Ferret Drive, Jackson 5997 ABN 78 921 444 556	Number _____ Date _____

Credit to
_____
_____
_____

Invoice no. ....
Invoice date   ....

Quantity	Description	Unit Price $	Amount $
- - - - - - -		- - - - - - - - - - -	- - - - - - - - - - -
- - - - - - -	GST included in this adjustment note $	- - - - - - - - - - -	- - - - - - - - - - -
Reasons for credit			

Ex. 2.6

```
┌ ─ ─ ─ ─ ─ ─ ─ ─ ─ ─ ─ ─ ─ ─ ─ ┐
        POS Daily Summary
    Date            ..

    Cash
    EFTPOS          ─ ─ ─ ─ ─ ─ ─ ─
    AMEX/Diners     ─ ─ ─ ─ ─ ─ ─ ─
                    ─ ─ ─ ─ ─ ─ ─ ─
    Total inc. GST
                    ─ ─ ─ ─ ─ ─ ─ ─
    GST included in
    Total
                    ─ ─ ─ ─ ─ ─ ─ ─
└ ─ ─ ─ ─ ─ ─ ─ ─ ─ ─ ─ ─ ─ ─ ─ ┘
```

Adjustment Note	B Black,	Number _____
	15 Greystone Road,	Date _____
	Jackson 5997	
	ABN 98 777 825 369	
Credit to		Invoice no. ....
_____		Invoice date ....
_____		
_____		

Description		Quantity	Unit Price (inc. GST)	Amount (inc. GST)
			$	$
	GST included in this adjustment note $_____			
Reasons for credit				

Receipt	Bunny's Pet Shop	Number __R55_____
		Date 9/7/2017

Received from _____

The sum of _____ dollars and

_____ cents

For _____

	$ _____ (inc. GST $ ___)
Discount	$ _____ (inc. GST $ ___)

Signed _____

No. 4762		
Date _____		No. 4762
To _____	Bank of Victoria	Stamp duty paid
For_____	Jackson West	
_____		Date _____
	Pay_____ or bearer	
	Balance	The sum of _____
	Deposits	
		$
	This cheque	
	Balance	_____

Ex. 2.6

Remittance advice	Bunny's Pet Shop 15 Ferret Drive, Jackson 5997 ABN 78 921 444 556				
To				Date _____	
Date Particulars	Reference	Debit	Credit	Balance	
		$	$	$	
- - - - - - - - - - - - - -	- - - - - - -	- - - - - - -	- - - - - - -	- - - - - - -	
- - - - - - - - - - - - - -	- - - - - - -	- - - - - - -	- - - - - - -	- - - - - - -	
- - - - - - - - - - - - - -	- - - - - - -	- - - - - - -	- - - - - - -	- - - - - - -	
- - - - - - - - - - - - - -	- - - - - - -	- - - - - - -	- - - - - - -	- - - - - - -	
- - - - - - - - - - - - - -	- - - - - - -	- - - - - - -	- - - - - - -	- - - - - - -	
Details of payment	**Balance owing**	$			
	less Discount	$			
	= Cheque amount	$			

Statement of account	Bunny's Pet Shop 15 Ferret Drive, Jackson 3998 ABN 78 921 444 556				
To					
			For period ending _____		
Date Particulars	Reference	Debit	Credit	Balance	
		$	$	$	
- - - - - - - - - - - - - -	- - - - - - -	- - - - - - -	- - - - - - -	- - - - - - -	
- - - - - - - - - - - - - -	- - - - - - -	- - - - - - -	- - - - - - -	- - - - - - -	
- - - - - - - - - - - - - -	- - - - - - -	- - - - - - -	- - - - - - -	- - - - - - -	
- - - - - - - - - - - - - -	- - - - - - -	- - - - - - -	- - - - - - -	- - - - - - -	
- - - - - - - - - - - - - -	- - - - - - -	- - - - - - -	- - - - - - -	- - - - - - -	
Terms					

Ex. 2.7   **Solution in textbook.**

Tax Invoice	Harfield Hardware Supply 1 Finch Street, Harfield 9445 ABN 22 411 511 611	Number _____ Date _____
Debit to		**Order no.** ....

Description	Quantity	Unit Price (inc. GST)	Amount (inc. GST)
		$	$

Adjustment Note	Harfield Hardware Supply 1 Finch Street, Harfield 9445 ABN 22 411 511 611	Number _____ Date _____
Credit to		**Invoice no.** .... **Invoice date** ....

Description	Quantity	Unit Price (inc. GST)	Amount (inc. GST)
		$	$
Reasons for credit			

Commonwealth Bank	**Commonwealth** Bank	**Deposit**
Commonwealth Bank of Australia	Commonwealth Bank of Australia	
Date _____		**Date** _____
Account Identification Number	Account Identification Number	Notes
		Coin
Account Name	Account Name	Cheques
		(see reverse)
$ _____ Teller	Paid in by (Signature) Teller	Total
Deposit Receipt		

Back of Deposit slip.

Commonwealth Bank

Commonwealth Bank of Australia

Proceeds of cheques will not be available until cleared

Details	Amount	Drawer	Bank	Branch	Amount
		1			
		2			
		3			
		4			
		5			
	$ _____				$ _____

Ex. 2.7   **Solution in textbook.**

Receipt	Harfield Hardware Supply	Number _____
		Date _____

Received from _____

The sum of _____ dollars and

_____ cents

For _____

$ _____

Discount $ _____ (inc. GST $)

Signed _____

No. 000004	**Commonwealth** Bank	No. 000004
Date _____	Commonwealth Bank of Australia	Stamp duty paid
To _____	**HARFIELD HARDWARE SUPPLY**	
For _____		Date _____
_____	Pay _____ or bearer	
	The sum of _____	

	Balance
	Deposits
	This cheque
	Balance

The sum of _____

_____ $ _____._____

_____

Statement of account	**Harfield Hardware Supply**
	1 Finch Street,
	Harfield 9445
	ABN 22 411 511 611

To

....

....

....

For period ending _____

Date	Particulars	Reference	Debit	Credit	Balance
			$	$	$

Terms

Ex. 2.8

Purchase order	A Sparks 61 Don Street, Westville ABN 44 111 222 000	Number _____ Date _____
To		

Quantity	Description	Estimated Price (inc. GST)
		$

Delivery by: **Method** _____

Date _____ **Authorised by** _____

Tax Invoice	**M Abe 473 Current Street, Southville ABN 66 000 111 999**	**Number** _____ **Date** _____
Debit to		**Order no.** ....

Description	Quantity	Unit Price	Amount (inc. GST)
		$	$
GST included in this invoice $_____			

Ex. 2.8

Delivery Docket	Number _____	Date _____

Deliver from   **M Abe**
                              473 Current St, Southville

Deliver to   _____
                          _____

The following goods:

Quantity	Description
- - - - - - - -	- -
- - - - - - - -	- -
- - - - - - - -	- -

Method of delivery _____
Received in good order and condition

_____
(Signature of receiver)

Adjustment Note	M Abe 473 Current Street, Southville ABN 66 000 111 999	Number _____ Date _____

Credit to
_____
_____
_____

Invoice no. ....
Invoice date   ....

Quantity	Description	Unit Price (inc. GST)	Amount (inc. GST)
		$	$
- - - - - - -	- - - - - - - - - - - - - - - - - - - -	- - - - - - - -	- - - - - - - -
- - - - - - -	- - - - - - - - - - - - - - - - - - - -	- - - - - - - -	- - - - - - - -
- - - - - - -	GST included in this adjustment note $ _____	- - - - - - - -	- - - - - - - -
Reasons for credit			

Ex. 2.9

Tax Invoice Debit to	G Bear 3 Downs Crescent Ringvale ABN 44 550 660 770		Number _____ Date _____ Order no. .... Delivery date ....

Description	Quantity	Unit Price (inc. GST) $	Amount (inc. GST) $
GST included in this invoice $_____			

Tax Invoice Debit to	Wolfe Industries Ltd 60 Dandenong Road Seville ABN 41 400 500 600		Number _____ Date _____ Order no. .... Delivery date ....

Description	Quantity	Unit Price (inc. GST) $	Amount (inc. GST) $
GST included in this invoice $_____			

No. 932516
Date *19/1/2016*
To *A Grey*
For *Rent*
(includes $_____ GST)

	Balance
	Deposits
	This cheque
	Balance

Ex. 2.9

Receipt	G Bear, 3 Downs Crescent Ringvale ABN 44 550 660 770	Number _____ Date _____

Received from _____

The sum of _____ dollars and

_____ cents

For _____

$ _____

Discount $ _____ (inc. GST $_____)

Signed _____

Adjustment Note	G Bear 3 Downs Crescent Ringvale ABN 44 550 660 770	Number _____ Date _____

Credit to

_____

_____

_____

Invoice no. ... .
Invoice date . .....

Quantity	Description	Unit Price (inc. GST)	Amount (inc. GST)
		$	$
	GST included in this adjustment note $_____		
Reasons for credit			

Ex. 2.10   Solution in textbook.

(a) _____

(b) _____

(c) _____

(d) _____

(e) _____

(f) _____

(g) _____

(h) _____

(i) _____

(j) _____

(k) _____

(l) _____

(m) _____

Ex. 2.11

(a) Two ways in which suppliers' invoices can be checked for accuracy and validity.

_____

_____

(b) Reasons for systematic filing of business documents

_____

_____

_____

_____

Ex. 2.12

(a) Accounting treatment of EFTPOS and credit card sales.

_____

_____

_____

_____

(b) How a business could utilise electronic banking facilities.

_____

_____

_____

_____

Ex. 2.13   Briefly describe the purpose of journals.

_____

_____

Ex. 2.14   Diagram of the accounting process.

_____

_____

_____

_____

_____

_____

_____

_____

_____

_____

_____

Ex. 2.15

(a) What is a 'special' journal?

_____

_____

(b) Name the different special journals.

_____

_____

_____

Ex. 2.16 Explain the meaning of the word 'posting' in relation to journals.

_____

_____

Ex. 2.17 Journals used to record credit transactions involving trading stock:

_____

_____

_____

_____

Ex. 2.18 Name the business documents that provide the source of information for these journals.

(a) _____

(b) _____

(c) _____

(d) _____

Ex. 2.19 Distinguish between:
(a) Sales return

_____

_____

(b) Sales allowance

_____

_____

_____

_____

_____

_____

_____

Ex. 2.20

E Singh, Used Car Dealer
Sales Journal

Date	Debtor	Fol	Ref	Sales	Sundries		GST collected	Accounts receivable control
					Amount	Account		

Ex. 2.21   Solution in textbook.

G Chapman, Sporting-goods Distributor
Sales Journal

Date	Debtor	Fol	Ref	Sales	Sundries		GST collected	Accounts receivable control
					Amount	Account		

Exercise 2.20 - 2.21

Ex. 2.22

Ivan's Wines and Spirits
Sales Journal

Date	Debtor	Fol	Ref	Sales		Sundries		GST	Accounts receivable control
				Wines	Spirits	Amount	Account	collected	

Ex. 2.23

Ace Parts
Sales Journal

Date	Debtor	Fol	Ref	Sales		Sundries		GST	Accounts receivable control
				Car parts	Truck parts	Amount	Account	collected	

Exercise 2.22 - 2.23

Ex. 2.24   Solution in textbook.

P Searle, Wholesaler
Purchases Journal

Date	Creditor	Fol	Ref	Purchases	Sundries		GST paid	Accounts payable control
					Amount	Account		

Ex. 2.25

Con's Menswear
Purchases Journal

Date	Creditor	Fol	Ref	Purchases			Sundries		GST paid	Accounts payable control
				Mens	Youths	Amount	Account			

Exercise 2.24 - 2.25

Ex. 2.26

Billie's Pastry Shop
Purchases Journal

Date	Creditor	Fol	Ref	Purchases		Sundries		GST paid	Accounts payable control
				Pies	Cakes	Amount	Account		

Ex. 2.27

E Singh, Used Car Dealer
Sales Returns and Allowances Journal

Date	Debtor	Fol	Ref	Sales returns	Sundries		GST collected	Accounts receivable control
					Amount	Account		

Ex. 2.28   Solution in textbook.

G Wanganeen, Sporting-goods Distributor
Sales Returns and Allowances Journal

Date	Debtor	Fol	Ref	Sales returns	Sundries		GST collected	Accounts receivable control
					Amount	Account		

Exercise 2.26 - 2.28

Ex. 2.29

Ivan's Wine and Spirits
Sales Returns and Allowances Journal

Date	Debtor	Fol	Ref	Sales returns		Sundries		GST collected	Accounts receivable control
				Wines	Spirits	Amount	Account		

Ex. 2.30

Ace Parts
Sales Returns and Allowances Journal

Date	Debtor	Fol	Ref	Sales returns		Sundries		GST collected	Accounts receivable control
				Car parts	Truck parts	Amount	Account		

Ex. 2.31   Solution in textbook.

P Searle, Wholesaler
Purchases Returns and Allowances Journal

Date	Creditor	Fol	Ref	Purchases returns	Sundries		GST paid	Accounts payable control
				Amount	Amount	Account		

Ex. 2.32

Con's Menswear
Purchases Returns and Allowances Journal

Date	Creditor	Fol	Ref	Purchases returns		Sundries		GST paid	Accounts payable control
				Menswear	Youthwear	Amount	Account		

Ex. 2.33

Billie's Pastry Shop
Purchases Returns and Allowances Journal

Date	Creditor	Fol	Ref	Purchases returns		Sundries		GST paid	Accounts payable control
				Pies	Cakes	Amount	Account		

Ex. 2.34

Bartlett's Electrical
Sales Journal

Date	Debtor	Fol	Ref	Sales	Sundries		GST collected	Accounts receivable control
					Amount	Account		

Exercise 2.32 - 2.34

Ex. 2.34

Bartlett's Electrical
Purchases Journal

Date	Creditor	Fol	Ref	Purchases	Sundries		GST paid	Accounts payable control
					Amount	Account		

Sales Returns and Allowances Journal

Date	Debtor	Fol	Ref	Sales returns	Sundries		GST collected	Accounts receivable control
					Amount	Account		

Purchases Returns and Allowances Journal

Date	Creditor	Fol	Ref	Purchases returns	Sundries		GST paid	Accounts payable control
					Amount	Account		

Exercise 2.34 (2)

Ex. 2.35

Cash sales of trading stock _____

Cash purchases of trading stock _____

Ex. 2.36   Source documents for:

(a) Cash Receipts Journal _____

(b) Cash Payments Journal

Ex. 2.37

E Singh, Used Car Dealer
Cash Receipts Journal

Date	Particulars	Fol	Ref	Discount expense			Accounts receivable control	Cash sales	Sundries		GST collected	Bank
				Accounts receivable control	Discount expense	GST collected			Amount	Account		

Exercise 2.35 - 2.37

Ex. 2.38

G Wanganeen, Sporting-goods Distributor
Cash Receipts Journal

| Date | Particulars | Fol | Ref | Discount expense | | | Cash | Sundries | | GST | Bank |
				Accounts receivable control	GST collected	Discount expense	Accounts receivable control	sales	Amount	Account	collected	

Exercise 2.38

To Trial Balance Workbook 6e

Ex. 2.39

Ivan's Wines and Spirits
Cash Receipts Journal

Date	Particulars	Fol	Ref	Discount expense			Accounts receivable control	Cash sales		Sundries		GST collected	Bank
				Accounts receivable control	GST collected	Discount expense		Wine	Spirits	Amount	Account		

Exercise 2.39

Ex. 2.40

Ace Parts
Cash Receipts Journal

| Date | Particulars | Fol | Ref | Discount expense | | | Accounts receivable control | Cash sales | | Sundries | | GST | Bank |
				Accounts receivable control	GST collected	Discount expense		Car	Truck	Amount	Account	collected	

Ex. 2.41

P Searle, Wholesaler
Cash Payments Journal

Date	Particulars	Fol	Ref	Discount income		Accounts payable control	Cash purchases	Wages	Sundries		GST paid	Bank
				Accounts payable control	Discount income	GST paid			Amount	Account		

Exercise 2.41

To Trial Balance Workbook 6e

Ex. 2.42

Con's Menswear
Cash Payments Journal

| Date | Particulars | Fol | Ref | Discount income | | | Accounts | Cash Purchases | | Wages | Sundries | | GST | Bank |
				Accounts payable control	GST paid	Discount income	payable control	Mens	Youths		Amount	Account	paid	

Exercise 2.42

To Trial Balance Workbook 6e

Ex. 2.43

Billie's Pastry Shop
Cash Payments Journal

Date	Particulars	Fol	Ref	Discount income			Accounts	Cash purchases		Wages	Sundries		GST	Bank
				Accounts payable control	GST paid	Discount income	payable control	Pies	Cakes		Amount	Account	paid	

Exercise 2.43

Ex. 2.44   Solution in textbook.

Mac's Cameras
Cash Receipts Journal

| Date | Particulars | Fol | Ref | Discount expense | | | Accounts receivable control | Cash sales | Sundries | | GST collected | Bank |
				Accounts receivable control	GST collected	Discount expense			Amount	Account		

Ex. 2.44   Solution in textbook.

Mac's Cameras
Cash Payments Journal

| Date | Particulars | Fol | Ref | Discount income | | | Accounts payable control | Cash purchases | Wages | Sundries | | GST | Bank |
				Accounts payable control	GST paid	Discount income				Amount	Account	paid	

To Trial Balance Workbook 6e

Ex. 2.45

Happy Hardware
Cash Receipts Journal

| Date | Particulars | Fol | Ref | Discount expense | | | Accounts receivable control | Cash sales | | Sundries | | GST | Bank |
				Accounts receivable	GST collected	Discount expense		KW	CR	Amount	Account	collected	

Exercise 2.45

Ex. 2.45

Happy Hardware
Cash Payments Journal

| Date | Particulars | Fol | Ref | Discount income | | | Accounts payable control | Cash purchases | | Wages | Sundries | | GST | Bank |
				Accounts payable control	GST paid	Discount Income		KW	CR		Amount	Account	paid	

Exercise 2.45 (2)

Ex. 2.46

Bartlett's Electrical
Cash Receipts Journal

| Date | Particulars | Fol | Ref | Discount expense | | | Accounts | Cash | Sundries | | GST | Bank |
				Accounts receivable control	GST collected	Discount expense	receivable control	sales	Amount	Account	collected	

Ex. 2.46

Bartlett's Electrical
Cash Payments Journal

| Date | Particulars | Fol | Ref | Discount income | | | Accounts | Cash | Wages | Sundries | | GST | Bank |
				Accounts payable control	GST paid	Discount income	payable control	purchases		Amount	Account	paid	

Exercise 2.46

Ex. 2.46

Bartlett's Electrical
Sales Journal

Date	Debtor	Fol	Ref	Sales	Sundries		GST collected	Accounts receivable control
					Amount	Account		

Ex. 2.46

Bartlett's Electrical
Purchases Journal

Date	Creditor	Fol	Ref	Purchases	Sundries		GST paid	Accounts payable control
					Amount	Account		

Ex. 2.46

Bartlett's Electrical
Sales Returns and Allowances Journal

Date	Debtor	Fol	Ref	Sales returns	Sundries		GST collected	Accounts receivable control
					Amount	Account		

Ex. 2.46

Bartlett's Electrical
Purchases Returns and Allowances Journal

Date	Creditor	Fol	Ref	Purchases returns	Sundries		GST paid	Accounts payable control
					Amount	Account		

Exercise 2.46 (2)

Ex. 2.47

Happy Hardware
Cash Receipts Journal

Date	Particulars	Fol	Ref	Discount expense			Accounts receivable control	Cash sales		Sundries			GST	Bank
				receivable control	GST collected	Discount expense		KW	CR	Amount	Account		collected	

Ex. 2.47

Happy Hardware
Cash Payments Journal

Date	Particulars	Fol	Ref	Discount income			Accounts payable control	Cash purchases		Wages	Sundries			GST	Bank
				Accounts payable control	GST paid	Discount income		KW	CR		Amount	Account		paid	

Exercise 2.47

Ex. 2.47

Happy Hardware
Sales Journal

Date	Debtor	Fol	Ref	Sales		Sundries		GST collected	Accounts receivable control
				KW	CR	Amount	Account		

Ex. 2.47

Happy Hardware
Purchases Journal

Date	Creditor	Fol	Ref	Purchases		Sundries		GST paid	Accounts payable control
				KW	CR	Amount	Account		

Ex. 2.47

Happy Hardware
Sales Returns and Allowances Journal

Date	Debtor	Fol	Ref	Sales returns		Sundries		GST collected	Accounts receivable control
				KW	CR	Amount	Account		

Ex. 2.47

Happy Hardware
Purchases Returns and Allowances Journal

Date	Creditor	Fol	Ref	Purchases returns		Sundries		GST paid	Accounts payable control
				KW	CR	Amount	Account		

Exercise 2.47 (2)

Ex. 2.48

(a) What is GST?

_____

_____

_____

(b) What is an input tax credit?

_____

_____

_____

_____

(c) How does a business calculate GST payable/refundable?

_____

_____

(d) Four examples of transactions not subject to GST.

_____

_____

_____

_____

_____

_____

_____

_____

_____

_____

_____

Ex. 2.49   Discuss the nature and purpose of the following.

(a) GST Collected Account

_____

_____

_____

(b) GST Paid Account

_____

_____

_____

Ex. 2.50   True or false

(a) _____

(b) _____

(c) _____

(d) _____

(e) _____

(f) _____

Ex. 2.51   List the seven types of journals and briefly describe types of transactions recorded in each.

Journal   Transaction type

1 _____

2 _____

3 _____

4 _____

5 _____

6 _____

7 _____

Ex. 2.52   Briefly explain the relationship between the journals and the ledgers.

_____

_____

Ex. 2.53   What is the purpose of the General Journal?

_____

_____

_____

Examples of General Journal transactions.

1 _____

2 _____

3 _____

Ex. 2.54   Journal used.

(a) _____

(b) _____

(c) _____

(d) _____

(e) _____

(f) _____

(g) _____

(h) _____

(i) _____

(j) _____

(k) _____

(l) _____

Ex. 2.55   **Wally's Video Sales**
                                  General Journal

Date	Particulars	Fol	Debit $	Credit $

Ex. 2.56   **Ivan's Wines and Spirits**
                                  General Journal

Date	Particulars	Fol	Debit $	Credit $

Ex. 2.57   **Con's Menswear**
                                  General Journal

Date	Particulars	Fol	Debit $	Credit $

Ex. 2.58

E Singh
General Journal

Date	Particulars	Fol	Debit $	Credit $

Ex. 2.59

G Chapman
General Journal

Date	Particulars	Fol	Debit $	Credit $

Ex. 2.60

I Muffdit
General Journal

Date	Particulars	Fol	Debit $	Credit $

Ex. 2.61

K Desanges
General Journal

Date	Particulars	Fol	Debit $	Credit $

Ex. 2.62 **Solution in textbook.**

I Jenkins
General Journal

Date	Particulars	Fol	Debit $	Credit $

Ex. 2.63   J Duff
                                                                          General Journal

Date	Particulars	Fol	Debit $	Credit $

Ex. 2.64

Billie's Pastry Shop
General Journal

Date	Particulars	Fol	Debit $	Credit $

Ex. 2.65

Stewart Bishop
General Journal

Date	Particulars	Fol	Debit $	Credit $

Ex. 2.65

Stewart Bishop
Cash Receipts Journal

| Date | Particulars | Fol | Ref | Discount expense | | | Accounts receivable control | Cash | Sundries | | GST | Bank |
				Accounts receivable control	GST collected	Discount expense		sales	Amount	Account	collected	

Ex. 2.65

Stewart Bishop
Cash Payments Journal

| Date | Particulars | Fol | Ref | Discount income | | | Accounts payable control | Cash | Wages | Sundries | | GST | Bank |
				Accounts payable control	GST paid	Discount income		purchases		Amount	Account	paid	

Exercise 2.65 (2)

Ex. 2.65

Stewart Bishop
Sales Journal

Date	Debtor	Fol	Ref	Sales	Sundries		GST collected	Accounts receivable control
					Amount	Account		

Ex. 2.65

Stewart Bishop
Purchases Journal

Date	Creditor	Fol	Ref	Purchases	Sundries		GST paid	Accounts payable control
					Amount	Account		

Ex. 2.65

Stewart Bishop
Sales Returns and Allowances Journal

Date	Debtor	Fol	Ref	Sales returns	Sundries		GST collected	Accounts receivable control
					Amount	Account		

Ex. 2.65

Stewart Bishop
Purchases Returns and Allowances Journal

Date	Creditor	Fol	Ref	Purchases returns	Sundries		GST paid	Accounts payable control
					Amount	Account		

Exercise 2.65 (3)

Ex. 2.66   Solution in textbook.

Mac's Cameras
General Journal

Date	Particulars	Fol	Debit $	Credit $

Ex. 2.66   Solution in textbook.

Mac's Cameras
Cash Receipts Journal

Date	Particulars	Fol	Ref	Discount expense			Accounts receivable control	Cash sales	Sundries		GST collected	Bank
				Accounts receivable control	GST collected	Discount expense			Amount	Account		

Ex. 2.66

Mac's Cameras
Cash Payments Journal

Date	Particulars	Fol	Ref	Discount income			Accounts payable control	Cash purchases	Wages	Sundries		GST paid	Bank
				Accounts payable control	GST paid	Discount income				Amount	Account		

Exercise 2.66 (2)

Ex. 2.66   Solution in textbook.

Mac's Cameras
Sales Journal

Date	Debtor	Fol	Ref	Sales	Sundries		GST collected	Accounts receivable control
					Amount	Account		

Ex. 2.66

Mac's Cameras
Purchases Journal

Date	Creditor	Fol	Ref	Purchases	Sundries		GST paid	Accounts payable control
					Amount	Account		

Ex. 2.66

Mac's Cameras
Sales Returns and Allowances Journal

Date	Debtor	Fol	Ref	Sales returns	Sundries		GST collected	Accounts receivable control
					Amount	Account		

Ex. 2.66

Mac's Cameras
Purchases Returns and Allowances Journal

Date	Creditor	Fol	Ref note no	Purchases returns	Sundries		GST paid	Accounts payable control
					Amount	Account		

Exercise 2.66 (3)

Ex. 2.67

Bartlett's Electrical
General Journal

Date	Particulars	Fol	Debit $	Credit $

Ex. 2.67

Bartlett's Electrical
Cash Receipts Journal

Date	Particulars	Fol	Ref	Discount expense			Accounts receivable control	Cash sales	Sundries		GST collected	Bank
				Accounts receivable control	GST collected	Discount expense			Amount	Account		

Ex. 2.67

Bartlett's Electrical
Cash Payments Journal

Date	Particulars	Fol	Ref	Discount income			Accounts payable control	Cash purchases	Wages	Sundries		GST paid	Bank
				Accounts payable control	GST paid	Discount income				Amount	Account		

Exercise 2.67 (2)

Ex. 2.67

Bartlett's Electrical
Sales Journal

Date	Debtor	Fol	Ref	Sales	Sundries		GST collected	Accounts receivable control
					Amount	Account		

Ex. 2.67

Bartlett's Electrical
Purchases Journal

Date	Creditor	Fol	Invoice number	Purchases	Sundries		GST paid	Accounts payable control
					Amount	Account		

Ex. 2.67

Bartlett's Electrical
Sales Returns and Allowances Journal

Date	Debtor	Fol	Adjustment note no.	Sales returns	Sundries		GST collected	Accounts receivable control
					Amount	Account		

Ex. 2.67

Bartlett's Electrical
Purchases Returns and Allowances Journal

Date	Creditor	Fol	Adjustment note no.	Purchases returns	Sundries		GST paid	Accounts payable control
					Amount	Account		

Exercise 2.67 (3)

Ex. 2.68

Happy Hardware
General Journal

Date	Particulars	Fol	Debit $	Credit $

Ex. 2.68

Happy Hardware
Cash Receipts Journal

Date	Particulars	Fol	Ref	Discount expense			Accounts receivable control	Cash sales		Sundries			GST	Bank
				Accounts receivable control	GST collected	Discount expense		KW	CR	Amount	Account		collected	

Ex. 2.68

Happy Hardware
Cash Payments Journal

Date	Particulars	Fol	Ref	Discount income			Accounts payable control	Cash purchases		Wages	Sundries			GST	Bank
				Accounts payable control	Discount income	GST paid		KW	CR		Amount	Account		paid	

Exercise 2.68 (2)

Ex. 2.68

Happy Hardware
Sales Journal

Date	Debtor	Fol	Ref	Sales		Sundries		GST collected	Accounts receivable control
				KW	CR	Amount	Account		

Ex. 2.68

Happy Hardware
Purchases Journal

Date	Creditor	Fol	Invoice number	Purchases		Sundries		GST paid	Accounts payable control
				KW	CR	Amount	Account		

Ex. 2.68

Happy Hardware
Sales Returns and Allowances Journal

Date	Debtor	Fol	Adjustment note no.	Sales returns		Sundries		GST collected	Accounts receivable control
				KW	CR	Amount	Account		

Ex. 2.68

Happy Hardware
Purchases Returns and Allowances Journal

Date	Creditor	Fol	Adjustment note no.	Purchases returns		Sundries		GST paid	Accounts payable control
				KW	CR	Amount	Account		

Exercise 2.68 (3)

Ex. 2.69

I Drill, Metal Fabricator
General Journal

Date	Particulars	Fol	Debit $	Credit $

Ex. 2.69

I Drill, Metal Fabricator
Sales and Services Journal

Date	Debtor	Fol	Ref	Services	Sundries Amount	Sundries Account	GST collected	Accounts receivable control

Ex. 2.69

I Drill, Metal Fabricator
Purchases and Supplies Journal

Date	Creditor	Fol	Ref	Supplies	Sundries Amount	Sundries Account	GST paid	Accounts payable control

Exercise 2.69

To Trial Balance Workbook 6e

Ex. 2.69

I Drill, Metal Fabricator
Cash Receipts Journal

Date	Particulars	Fol	Ref	Discount expense			Accounts receivable control	Cash services	Sundries		GST collected	Bank
				Accounts receivable control	GST collected	Discount expense			Amount	Account		

Ex. 2.69

I Drill, Metal Fabricator
Cash Payments Journal

Date	Particulars	Fol	Ref	Discount income			Accounts payable control	Supplies	Wages	Sundries		GST paid	Bank
				Accounts payable control	GST paid	Discount income				Amount	Account		

Exercise 2.69 (2)

Ex. 2.70

Sleep's Relaxation Centre
General Journal

Date	Particulars	Fol	Debit $	Credit $

Ex. 2.70

Sleep's Relaxation Centre
Cash Receipts Journal

Date	Particulars	Fol	Ref	Service fees			Sundries		GST collected	Bank
				Massage	Solarium	Amount	Account			

Exercise 2.70

Ex. 2.70

Sleep's Relaxation Centre
Cash Payments Journal

Date	Particulars	Fol	Cheque number	Rent expense	Advertising	Wages	Laundry	Accounts payable control	Sundries		GST paid	Bank
									Amount	Account		

Ex. 2.70

Sleep's Relaxation Centre
Purchases and Supplies Journal

Date	Creditor	Fol	Ref	Supplies		Sundries		GST paid	Accounts payable control
				Massage	Solarium	Amount	Account		

Ex. 2.70

Sleep's Relaxation Centre
Sales and Services Journal

Date	Creditor	Fol	Ref	Services		Sundries		GST collected	Accounts receivable control
				Massage	Solarium	Amount	Account		

Exercise 2.70 (2)

Ex. 2.71   Solution in textbook.

Happy Nappies
General Journal

Date	Particulars	Fol	Debit $	Credit $

Ex. 2.71

Happy Nappies
Sales and Services Journal

Date	Debtor	Fol	Ref	Services	Amount	Sundries Account	GST collected	Accounts receivable control

Ex. 2.71 Solution in textbook.

Happy Nappies
Purchases and Supplies Journal

Date	Creditor	Fol	Ref	Purchases	Sundries		GST paid	Accounts payable control
					Amount	Account		

Ex. 2.71

Happy Nappies
Cash Receipts Journal

Date	Particulars	Fol	Ref	Discount expense			Accounts receivable control	Cash services	Sundries		GST collected	Bank
				Accounts receivable control	Discount expense	GST collected			Amount	Account		

Ex. 2.71

Happy Nappies
Cash Payments Journal

Date	Particulars	Fol	Ref	Discount income			Accounts payable control	Cash purchases	Wages	Sundries		GST paid	Bank
				Accounts payable control	Discount income	GST paid				Amount	Account		

Exercise 2.71 (2)

Ex. 3.1

M Thompson
General Ledger
Stock Account

Date	Particulars	Fol	Debit $	Credit $	Balance $

Land and Buildings Account

Date	Particulars	Fol	Debit $	Credit $	Balance $

Motor Vehicle Account

Date	Particulars	Fol	Debit $	Credit $	Balance $

Furniture and Fittings Account

Date	Particulars	Fol	Debit $	Credit $	Balance $

Mortgage Loan on Land and Buildings Account

Date	Particulars	Fol	Debit $	Credit $	Balance $

Bank Overdraft Account

Date	Particulars	Fol	Debit $	Credit $	Balance $

Capital – M Thompson Account

Date	Particulars	Fol	Debit $	Credit $	Balance $

Ex. 3.2

K Hinkley
General Ledger
Late Fees Expense Account

Date	Particulars	Fol	Debit $	Credit $	Balance $

GST Paid Account

Date	Particulars	Fol	Debit $	Credit $	Balance $

Accounts Payable Control Account

Date	Particulars	Fol	Debit $	Credit $	Balance $

Motor Vehicle Account

Date	Particulars	Fol	Debit $	Credit $	Balance $

Capital – K Hinkley Account

Date	Particulars	Fol	Debit $	Credit $	Balance $

Drawings – K Hinkley Account

Date	Particulars	Fol	Debit $	Credit $	Balance $

Purchases Account

Date	Particulars	Fol	Debit $	Credit $	Balance $

Bad Debts Account

Date	Particulars	Fol	Debit $	Credit $	Balance $

GST Collected Account

Date	Particulars	Fol	Debit $	Credit $	Balance $

Ex. 3.2

K Hinkley
General Ledger
Accounts Receivable Control Account

Date	Particulars	Fol	Debit $	Credit $	Balance $

Sales Account

Date	Particulars	Fol	Debit $	Credit $	Balance $

Late Fees Income Account

Date	Particulars	Fol	Debit $	Credit $	Balance $

Ex. 3.3

E Singh, Used Car Dealer
General Ledger
Accounts Receivable Control Account

Date	Particulars	Fol	Debit $	Credit $	Balance $

GST Collected Account

Date	Particulars	Fol	Debit $	Credit $	Balance $

Discount Expense Account

Date	Particulars	Fol	Debit $	Credit $	Balance $

Sales Account

Date	Particulars	Fol	Debit $	Credit $	Balance $

Capital – E Singh Account

Date	Particulars	Fol	Debit $	Credit $	Balance $

Commission Income Account

Date	Particulars	Fol	Debit $	Credit $	Balance $

Cash at Bank Account

Date	Particulars	Fol	Debit $	Credit $	Balance $

Ex. 3.4   Solution in textbook.

J Bartel, Sporting-goods Distributor
General Ledger
Discount Expense Account

Date	Particulars	Fol	Debit $	Credit $	Balance $

Accounts Receivable Control Account

Date	Particulars	Fol	Debit $	Credit $	Balance $

Sales Account

Date	Particulars	Fol	Debit $	Credit $	Balance $

Motor Vehicles Account

Date	Particulars	Fol	Debit $	Credit $	Balance $

GST Collected Account

Date	Particulars	Fol	Debit $	Credit $	Balance $

Capital – J Bartel Account

Date	Particulars	Fol	Debit $	Credit $	Balance $

Cash at Bank Account

Date	Particulars	Fol	Debit $	Credit $	Balance $

Commission Income Account

Date	Particulars	Fol	Debit $	Credit $	Balance $

Sale of Non-current Assets Account

Date	Particulars	Fol	Debit $	Credit $	Balance $

Ex. 3.5

Ivan's Wines and Spirits
General Ledger
Discount Expense Account

Date	Particulars	Fol	Debit $	Credit $	Balance $

Accounts Receivable Control Account

Date	Particulars	Fol	Debit $	Credit $	Balance $

Sales – Wines Account

Date	Particulars	Fol	Debit $	Credit $	Balance $

Sales – Spirits Account

Date	Particulars	Fol	Debit $	Credit $	Balance $

Capital – I Brown Account

Date	Particulars	Fol	Debit $	Credit $	Balance $

Rent Income Account

Date	Particulars	Fol	Debit $	Credit $	Balance $

Office Equipment Account

Date	Particulars	Fol	Debit $	Credit $	Balance $

Cash at Bank Account

Date	Particulars	Fol	Debit $	Credit $	Balance $

GST Collected Account

Date	Particulars	Fol	Debit $	Credit $	Balance $

Sale of Non-current Assets Account

Date	Particulars	Fol	Debit $	Credit $	Balance $

Ex. 3.6

P Shaw, Wholesaler
General Ledger
Accounts Payable Control Account

Date	Particulars	Fol	Debit $	Credit $	Balance $

Discount Income Account

Date	Particulars	Fol	Debit $	Credit $	Balance $

Purchases Account

Date	Particulars	Fol	Debit $	Credit $	Balance $

Wages Account

Date	Particulars	Fol	Debit $	Credit $	Balance $

Advertising Account

Date	Particulars	Fol	Debit $	Credit $	Balance $

Drawings – P Shaw Account

Date	Particulars	Fol	Debit $	Credit $	Balance $

Office Expenses Account

Date	Particulars	Fol	Debit $	Credit $	Balance $

Ex. 3.6

P Shaw Wholesaler
General Ledger

:aning Acco

Date	Particulars	Fol	Debit $	Credit $	Balance $

Cash at Bank Account

Date	Particulars	Fol	Debit $	Credit $	Balance $

GST Collected Account

Date	Particulars	Fol	Debit $	Credit $	Balance $

GST Paid Account

Date	Particulars	Fol	Debit $	Credit $	Balance $

Ex. 3.7

Con's Menswear
General Ledger
Accounts Payable Control Account

Date	Particulars	Fol	Debit $	Credit $	Balance $

Discount Income Account

Date	Particulars	Fol	Debit $	Credit $	Balance $

Loan From OFI Ltd Account

Date	Particulars	Fol	Debit $	Credit $	Balance $

Purchases – Menswear Account

Date	Particulars	Fol	Debit $	Credit $	Balance $

Purchases – Youthswear Account

Date	Particulars	Fol	Debit $	Credit $	Balance $

Wages Account

Date	Particulars	Fol	Debit $	Credit $	Balance $

Drawings – C Constantinou Account

Date	Particulars	Fol	Debit $	Credit $	Balance $

Ex. 3.7

Con's Menswear
General Ledger
Office Equipment Account

Date	Particulars	Fol	Debit $	Credit $	Balance $

GST Paid Account

Date	Particulars	Fol	Debit $	Credit $	Balance $

Cash at Bank Account

Date	Particulars	Fol	Debit $	Credit $	Balance $

Ex. 3.8

E Betts, Used Car Dealer
General Ledger
Accounts Receivable Control Account

Date	Particulars	Fol	Debit $	Credit $	Balance $

Sales Account

Date	Particulars	Fol	Debit $	Credit $	Balance $

Repair Income Account

Date	Particulars	Fol	Debit $	Credit $	Balance $

GST Collected Account

Date	Particulars	Fol	Debit $	Credit $	Balance $

Ex. 3.9

G Wanganeen, Sporting-goods Distributor
General Ledger
Accounts Receivable Control Account

Date	Particulars	Fol	Debit $	Credit $	Balance $

Sales Account

Date	Particulars	Fol	Debit $	Credit $	Balance $

Repairs Income Account

Date	Particulars	Fol	Debit $	Credit $	Balance $

GST Collected Account

Date	Particulars	Fol	Debit $	Credit $	Balance $

Ex. 3.10

Ace Parts
General Ledger
Sales – Car Parts Account

Date	Particulars	Fol	Debit $	Credit $	Balance $

Sales – Truck Parts Account

Date	Particulars	Fol	Debit $	Credit $	Balance $

Delivery Fees Income Account

Date	Particulars	Fol	Debit $	Credit $	Balance $

GST Collected Account

Date	Particulars	Fol	Debit $	Credit $	Balance $

Accounts Receivable Control Account

Date	Particulars	Fol	Debit $	Credit $	Balance $

Ex. 3.11

P Shaw, Wholesaler
General Ledger
Purchases Account

Date	Particulars	Fol	Debit $	Credit $	Balance $

Insurance Account

Date	Particulars	Fol	Debit $	Credit $	Balance $

Shop Fittings Account

Date	Particulars	Fol	Debit $	Credit $	Balance $

GST Paid Account

Date	Particulars	Fol	Debit $	Credit $	Balance $

Accounts Payable Control Account

Date	Particulars	Fol	Debit $	Credit $	Balance $

Ex. 3.12

Con's Menswear
General Ledger
Purchases – Menswear Account

Date	Particulars	Fol	Debit $	Credit $	Balance $

Purchases – Youthswear Account

Date	Particulars	Fol	Debit $	Credit $	Balance $

Telephone and Internet Account

Date	Particulars	Fol	Debit $	Credit $	Balance $

GST Paid Account

Date	Particulars	Fol	Debit $	Credit $	Balance $

Accounts Payable Control Account

Date	Particulars	Fol	Debit $	Credit $	Balance $

Ex. 3.13

E Betts, Used Car Dealer
General Ledger
Sales Returns and Allowances Account

Date	Particulars	Fol	Debit $	Credit $	Balance $

GST Collected Account

Date	Particulars	Fol	Debit $	Credit $	Balance $

Accounts Receivable Control Account

Date	Particulars	Fol	Debit $	Credit $	Balance $

Ex. 3.14

G Wanganeen, Sporting-goods Distributor
General Ledger
Sales Returns and Allowances Account

Date	Particulars	Fol	Debit $	Credit $	Balance $

Repairs Income Account

Date	Particulars	Fol	Debit $	Credit $	Balance $

GST Collected Account

Date	Particulars	Fol	Debit $	Credit $	Balance $

Accounts Receiveable Control Account

Date	Particulars	Fol	Debit $	Credit $	Balance $

Ex. 3.15

Chapman's Wines and Spirits
General Ledger
Sales Returns and Allowances (Wines) Account

Date	Particulars	Fol	Debit $	Credit $	Balance $

Sales Returns and Allowances (Spirits) Account

Date	Particulars	Fol	Debit $	Credit $	Balance $

GST Collected Account

Date	Particulars	Fol	Debit $	Credit $	Balance $

Accounts Receivable Control Account

Date	Particulars	Fol	Debit $	Credit $	Balance $

Ex. 3.16

P Searle, Wholesaler
General Ledger
Acounts Payable Control Account

Date	Particulars	Fol	Debit $	Credit $	Balance $

Purchases Returns and Allowances Account

Date	Particulars	Fol	Debit $	Credit $	Balance $

Insurance Account

Date	Particulars	Fol	Debit $	Credit $	Balance $

GST Paid Account

Date	Particulars	Fol	Debit $	Credit $	Balance $

Ex. 3.17

Billie's Pastry Shop
General Ledger
Accounts Payable Control Account

Date	Particulars	Fol	Debit $	Credit $	Balance $

Office Furniture Account

Date	Particulars	Fol	Debit $	Credit $	Balance $

Purchases Returns and Allowances (Pies) Account

Date	Particulars	Fol	Debit $	Credit $	Balance $

Purchases Returns and Allowances (Cakes) Account

Date	Particulars	Fol	Debit $	Credit $	Balance $

GST Paid Account

Date	Particulars	Fol	Debit $	Credit $	Balance $

Ex. 3.18   **Procedure used when posting all journals to the General Ledger at the end of the month.**

_____

_____

_____

_____

_____

_____

_____

_____

_____

_____

_____

_____

_____

Ex. 3.19   Solution in textbook.

Bright Spark
General Ledger
Stock Account

Date	Particulars	Fol	Debit $	Credit $	Balance $

Cash at Bank Account

Date	Particulars	Fol	Debit $	Credit $	Balance $

Premises Account

Date	Particulars	Fol	Debit $	Credit $	Balance $

Mortgage Loan on Premises Account

Date	Particulars	Fol	Debit $	Credit $	Balance $

Loan from B Burns Account

Date	Particulars	Fol	Debit $	Credit $	Balance $

Capital – B Spark Account

Date	Particulars	Fol	Debit $	Credit $	Balance $

Drawings – B Spark Account

Date	Particulars	Fol	Debit $	Credit $	Balance $

Purchases Account

Date	Particulars	Fol	Debit $	Credit $	Balance $

Ex. 3.19   Solution in textbook.

Bright Spark
General Ledger
GST Paid Account

Date	Particulars	Fol	Debit $	Credit $	Balance $

Accounts Receivable Control Account

Date	Particulars	Fol	Debit $	Credit $	Balance $

GST Collected Account

Date	Particulars	Fol	Debit $	Credit $	Balance $

Discount Expense Account

Date	Particulars	Fol	Debit $	Credit $	Balance $

Sales Account

Date	Particulars	Fol	Debit $	Credit $	Balance $

Commission Income Account

Date	Particulars	Fol	Debit $	Credit $	Balance $

Ex. 3.19   Solution in textbook.

Bright Spark
General Ledger
Accounts Payable Control Account

Date	Particulars	Fol	Debit $	Credit $	Balance $

Discount Income Account

Date	Particulars	Fol	Debit $	Credit $	Balance $

Wages Account

Date	Particulars	Fol	Debit $	Credit $	Balance $

Sales Returns and Allowances Account

Date	Particulars	Fol	Debit $	Credit $	Balance $

Sale of Non-current Assets Account

Date	Particulars	Fol	Debit $	Credit $	Balance $

Office Equipment Account

Date	Particulars	Fol	Debit $	Credit $	Balance $

Advertising Account

Date	Particulars	Fol	Debit $	Credit $	Balance $

Purchases Returns and Allowances Account

Date	Particulars	Fol	Debit $	Credit $	Balance $

Ex. 3.19   Solution in textbook.

Bright Spark
Trial Balance as at 31 July 2017

Account name	Debit $	Credit $

Ex. 3.20 (a) and (b)

Mac's Cameras
General Ledger
A1 Cash at Bank Account

Date	Particulars	Fol	Debit $	Credit $	Balance $

A2 Accounts Receivable Control Account

Date	Particulars	Fol	Debit $	Credit $	Balance $

A3 Land and Buildings Account

Date	Particulars	Fol	Debit $	Credit $	Balance $

A4 Motor Vehicles Account

Date	Particulars	Fol	Debit $	Credit $	Balance $

A5 Stock Account

Date	Particulars	Fol	Debit $	Credit $	Balance $

A6 GST Paid Account

Date	Particulars	Fol	Debit $	Credit $	Balance $

Ex. 3.20

Mac's Cameras
General Ledger
L1 Accounts Payable Control Account

Date	Particulars	Fol	Debit $	Credit $	Balance $

L2 Mortgage Loan Account

Date	Particulars	Fol	Debit $	Credit $	Balance $

L3 GST Collected Account

Date	Particulars	Fol	Debit $	Credit $	Balance $

OE1 Capital – C Mackintosh Account

Date	Particulars	Fol	Debit $	Credit $	Balance $

OE2 Drawings – C Mackintosh Account

Date	Particulars	Fol	Debit $	Credit $	Balance $

I1 Sales Account

Date	Particulars	Fol	Debit $	Credit $	Balance $

I1A Sales Returns and Allowances Account

Date	Particulars	Fol	Debit $	Credit $	Balance $

Ex. 3.20

Mac's Cameras
General Ledger
I2 Interest Income Account

Date	Particulars	Fol	Debit $	Credit $	Balance $

I3 Discount Income Account

Date	Particulars	Fol	Debit $	Credit $	Balance $

I4 Late Fees Income Account

Date	Particulars	Fol	Debit $	Credit $	Balance $

I5 Delivery Income Account

Date	Particulars	Fol	Debit $	Credit $	Balance $

E1 Purchases Account

Date	Particulars	Fol	Debit $	Credit $	Balance $

E1A Purchases Returns and Allowances Account

Date	Particulars	Fol	Debit $	Credit $	Balance $

E2 Discount Expense Account

Date	Particulars	Fol	Debit $	Credit $	Balance $

E3 Wages Account

Date	Particulars	Fol	Debit $	Credit $	Balance $

E4 Insurance Account

Date	Particulars	Fol	Debit $	Credit $	Balance $

Ex. 3.20

Mac's Cameras
General Ledger
E5 Bad Debts Account

Date	Particulars	Fol	Debit $	Credit $	Balance $

E6 Repairs Account

Date	Particulars	Fol	Debit $	Credit $	Balance $

E7 Merchant Fees Expense Account

Date	Particulars	Fol	Debit $	Credit $	Balance $

Ex. 3.20 (c)

Mac's Cameras
Trial Balance as at 31 January 2019

Account name	Debit $	Credit $

Ex. 3.21   Schmidt's Electrical
                                           General Ledger
                                   001 Cash at Bank Account

Date	Particulars	Fol	Debit $	Credit $	Balance $

002 Accounts Receivable Control Account

Date	Particulars	Fol	Debit $	Credit $	Balance $

003 Stock Account

Date	Particulars	Fol	Debit $	Credit $	Balance $

004 Motor Vehicles Account

Date	Particulars	Fol	Debit $	Credit $	Balance $

005 Furniture and Fittings Account

Date	Particulars	Fol	Debit $	Credit $	Balance $

006 Office Equipment Account

Date	Particulars	Fol	Debit $	Credit $	Balance $

007 Loan to AB Investments Account

Date	Particulars	Fol	Debit $	Credit $	Balance $

Ex. 3.21

Schmidt's Electrical
General Ledger
008 GST Paid Account

Date	Particulars	Fol	Debit $	Credit $	Balance $

101 Accounts Payable Control Account

Date	Particulars	Fol	Debit $	Credit $	Balance $

102 GST Collected Account

Date	Particulars	Fol	Debit $	Credit $	Balance $

201 Capital – N Schmidt Account

Date	Particulars	Fol	Debit $	Credit $	Balance $

Ex. 3.21

Schmidt's Electrical
General Ledger
202 Drawings – N Schmidt Account

Date	Particulars	Fol	Debit $	Credit $	Balance $

301 Sales Account

Date	Particulars	Fol	Debit $	Credit $	Balance $

302 Sales Returns and Allowances Account

Date	Particulars	Fol	Debit $	Credit $	Balance $

304 Discount Income Account

Date	Particulars	Fol	Debit $	Credit $	Balance $

305 Interest Income Account

Date	Particulars	Fol	Debit $	Credit $	Balance $

306 Sale of Non-current Assets Account

Date	Particulars	Fol	Debit $	Credit $	Balance $

401 Purchases Account

Date	Particulars	Fol	Debit $	Credit $	Balance $

402 Purchases Returns and Allowances Account

Date	Particulars	Fol	Debit $	Credit $	Balance $

Ex. 3.21

Schmidt's Electrical
General Ledger
403 Discount Expense Account

Date	Particulars	Fol	Debit $	Credit $	Balance $

404 Stationery Expense Account

Date	Particulars	Fol	Debit $	Credit $	Balance $

405 Bad Debts Account

Date	Particulars	Fol	Debit $	Credit $	Balance $

406 Wages Account

Date	Particulars	Fol	Debit $	Credit $	Balance $

407 Repairs Account

Date	Particulars	Fol	Debit $	Credit $	Balance $

408 Late Fees Expense Account

Date	Particulars	Fol	Debit $	Credit $	Balance $

411 Merchant Fees Expense Account

Date	Particulars	Fol	Debit $	Credit $	Balance $

Ex. 3.21

Schmidt's Electrical
Trial Balance as at 31 July 2017

Account name	Debit $	Credit $

Ex. 3.22   **Happy Hardware**
General Ledger
1.1 Cash at Bank Account

Date	Particulars	Fol	Debit $	Credit $	Balance $

1.2 Accounts Receivable Control Account

Date	Particulars	Fol	Debit $	Credit $	Balance $

1.3 Stock – Kitchenware Account

Date	Particulars	Fol	Debit $	Credit $	Balance $

1.4 Stock – Crockery Account

Date	Particulars	Fol	Debit $	Credit $	Balance $

1.5 Motor Vehicles Account

Date	Particulars	Fol	Debit $	Credit $	Balance $

1.6 Premises Account

Date	Particulars	Fol	Debit $	Credit $	Balance $

1.7 Furniture and Fittings Account

Date	Particulars	Fol	Debit $	Credit $	Balance $

Ex. 3.22

Happy Hardware
General Ledger
1.8 GST Paid Account

Date	Particulars	Fol	Debit $	Credit $	Balance $

2.1 Accounts Payable Control Account

Date	Particulars	Fol	Debit $	Credit $	Balance $

2.2 Mortgage Loan on Premises Account

Date	Particulars	Fol	Debit $	Credit $	Balance $

2.3 GST Collected Account

Date	Particulars	Fol	Debit $	Credit $	Balance $

3.1 Capital – R Ratnayake Account

Date	Particulars	Fol	Debit $	Credit $	Balance $

Ex. 3.22

Happy Hardware
General Ledger
3.2 Drawings – R Ratnayake Account

Date	Particulars	Fol	Debit $	Credit $	Balance $

4.1 Sales – Kitchenware Account

Date	Particulars	Fol	Debit $	Credit $	Balance $

4.2 Sales – Crockery Account

Date	Particulars	Fol	Debit $	Credit $	Balance $

4.3 Sales Returns and Allowances – Kitchenware Account

Date	Particulars	Fol	Debit $	Credit $	Balance $

4.4 Sales Returns and Allowances – Crockery Account

Date	Particulars	Fol	Debit $	Credit $	Balance $

4.5 Discount Income Account

Date	Particulars	Fol	Debit $	Credit $	Balance $

4.6 Commission Income Account

Date	Particulars	Fol	Debit $	Credit $	Balance $

4.7 Delivery Income Account

Date	Particulars	Fol	Debit $	Credit $	Balance $

5.1 Purchases – Kitchenware Account

Date	Particulars	Fol	Debit $	Credit $	Balance $

Ex. 3.22

Happy Hardware
General Ledger
5.2 Purchases – Crockery Account

Date	Particulars	Fol	Debit $	Credit $	Balance $

5.3 Purchases Returns and Allowances – Kitchenware Account

Date	Particulars	Fol	Debit $	Credit $	Balance $

5.5 Discount Expense Account

Date	Particulars	Fol	Debit $	Credit $	Balance $

5.6 Wages Account

Date	Particulars	Fol	Debit $	Credit $	Balance $

5.7 Repairs Account

Date	Particulars	Fol	Debit $	Credit $	Balance $

5.8 Bad Debts Account

Date	Particulars	Fol	Debit $	Credit $	Balance $

5.9 Municipal Rates Account

Date	Particulars	Fol	Debit $	Credit $	Balance $

Ex. 3.22

Happy Hardware
Trial Balance as at 31 July 2019

Account name	Debit $	Credit $

Ex. 3.23   **Laura Bangle**
                                         General Journal

Date	Particulars	Fol	Debit $	Credit $

Ex. 3.23

Laura Bangle
Cash Receipts Journal

| Date | Particulars | Fol | Ref | Discount expense | | | Accounts | Cash | Sundries | | GST | Bank |
				Accounts receivable control	GST collected	Discount expense	receivable control	sales	Amount	Account	collected	

Ex. 3.23

Laura Bangle
Cash Payments Journal

| Date | Particulars | Fol | Ref | Discount income | | | Accounts | Cash | Wages | Sundries | | GST | Bank |
				Accounts payable control	GST paid	Discount income	payable control	purchases		Amount	Account	paid	

Exercise 3.23 (2)

Ex. 3.23

Laura Bangle
Sales Journal

Date	Debtor	Fol	Ref	Sales	Sundries		GST collected	Accounts receivable control
					Amount	Account		

Ex. 3.23

Laura Bangle
Purchases Journal

Date	Creditor	Fol	Ref	Purchases	Sundries		GST paid	Accounts payable control
					Amount	Account		

Ex. 3.23

Laura Bangle
Sales Returns and Allowances Journal

Date	Debtor	Fol	Ref	Sales returns	Sundries		GST collected	Accounts receivable control
					Amount	Account		

Ex. 3.23

Laura Bangle
Purchases Returns and Allowances Journal

Date	Creditor	Fol	Ref	Purchases returns	Sundries		GST paid	Accounts payable control
					Amount	Account		

Exercise 3.23 (3)

Ex. 3.23

Laura Bangle
General Ledger
Cash at Bank Account

Date	Particulars	Fol	Debit $	Credit $	Balance $

Stock Account

Date	Particulars	Fol	Debit $	Credit $	Balance $

Vehicle Account

Date	Particulars	Fol	Debit $	Credit $	Balance $

Loan from Witch Bank Account

Date	Particulars	Fol	Debit $	Credit $	Balance $

Capital – L Bangle Account

Date	Particulars	Fol	Debit $	Credit $	Balance $

Drawings – L Bangle Account

Date	Particulars	Fol	Debit $	Credit $	Balance $

Purchases Account

Date	Particulars	Fol	Debit $	Credit $	Balance $

GST Paid Account

Date	Particulars	Fol	Debit $	Credit $	Balance $

Ex. 3.23

Laura Bangle
General Ledger
Accounts Receivable Control Account

Date	Particulars	Fol	Debit $	Credit $	Balance $

GST Collected Account

Date	Particulars	Fol	Debit $	Credit $	Balance $

Discount Expense Account

Date	Particulars	Fol	Debit $	Credit $	Balance $

Sales Account

Date	Particulars	Fol	Debit $	Credit $	Balance $

Commission Income Account

Date	Particulars	Fol	Debit $	Credit $	Balance $

Accounts Payable Control Account

Date	Particulars	Fol	Debit $	Credit $	Balance $

Discount Income Account

Date	Particulars	Fol	Debit $	Credit $	Balance $

Ex. 3.23

Laura Bangle
General Ledger
Wages Account

Date	Particulars	Fol	Debit $	Credit $	Balance $

Rent Expense Account

Date	Particulars	Fol	Debit $	Credit $	Balance $

Repair Income Account

Date	Particulars	Fol	Debit $	Credit $	Balance $

Furniture Account

Date	Particulars	Fol	Debit $	Credit $	Balance $

Advertising Account

Date	Particulars	Fol	Debit $	Credit $	Balance $

Sales Returns and Allowances Account

Date	Particulars	Fol	Debit $	Credit $	Balance $

Purchases Returns and Allowances Account

Date	Particulars	Fol	Debit $	Credit $	Balance $

Ex. 3.23   **Laura Bangle**
                                Trial Balance as at 31 May 2019

Account name	Debit $	Credit $

Ex. 3.24

I Drill
General Ledger
Drawings – I Drill Account

Date	Particulars	Fol	Debit $	Credit $	Balance $

Supplies Account

Date	Particulars	Fol	Debit $	Credit $	Balance $

GST Paid Account

Date	Particulars	Fol	Debit $	Credit $	Balance $

Accounts Receivable Control Account

Date	Particulars	Fol	Debit $	Credit $	Balance $

Service Fees Account

Date	Particulars	Fol	Debit $	Credit $	Balance $

Capital – I Drill Account

Date	Particulars	Fol	Debit $	Credit $	Balance $

GST Collected Account

Date	Particulars	Fol	Debit $	Credit $	Balance $

Cash at Bank Account

Date	Particulars	Fol	Debit $	Credit $	Balance $

Ex. 3.24

I Drill
General Ledger
Wages Account

Date	Particulars	Fol	Debit $	Credit $	Balance $

Repairs Account

Date	Particulars	Fol	Debit $	Credit $	Balance $

Lease – Premises Account

Date	Particulars	Fol	Debit $	Credit $	Balance $

Equipment Account

Date	Particulars	Fol	Debit $	Credit $	Balance $

Furniture Account

Date	Particulars	Fol	Debit $	Credit $	Balance $

Insurance Account

Date	Particulars	Fol	Debit $	Credit $	Balance $

Accounts Payable Control Account

Date	Particulars	Fol	Debit $	Credit $	Balance $

Ex. 3.24

I Drill
Trial Balance as at 31 May 2016

Account name	Debit $	Credit $

Ex. 3.25

Sleep's Relaxation Centre
General Ledger
Equipment Account

Date	Particulars	Fol	Debit $	Credit $	Balance $

Capital – L Sleep Account

Date	Particulars	Fol	Debit $	Credit $	Balance $

Laundry Expenses Account

Date	Particulars	Fol	Debit $	Credit $	Balance $

GST Paid Account

Date	Particulars	Fol	Debit $	Credit $	Balance $

Wages Account

Date	Particulars	Fol	Debit $	Credit $	Balance $

Service Fees – Massage Account

Date	Particulars	Fol	Debit $	Credit $	Balance $

Service Fees – Solarium Account

Date	Particulars	Fol	Debit $	Credit $	Balance $

GST Collected Account

Date	Particulars	Fol	Debit $	Credit $	Balance $

Ex. 3.25

Sleep's Relaxation Centre
General Ledger
Cash at Bank Account

Date	Particulars	Fol	Debit $	Credit $	Balance $

Accounts Payable Control Account

Date	Particulars	Fol	Debit $	Credit $	Balance $

Rent Expense Account

Date	Particulars	Fol	Debit $	Credit $	Balance $

Advertising Account

Date	Particulars	Fol	Debit $	Credit $	Balance $

Cleaning Expenses Account

Date	Particulars	Fol	Debit $	Credit $	Balance $

Accounts Receivable Control Account

Date	Particulars	Fol	Debit $	Credit $	Balance $

Accounting Fees Account

Date	Particulars	Fol	Debit $	Credit $	Balance $

Insurance Account

Date	Particulars	Fol	Debit $	Credit $	Balance $

Telephone Account

Date	Particulars	Fol	Debit $	Credit $	Balance $

Ex. 3.25

Sleep's Relaxation Centre
Trial Balance as at 30 June 2017

Account name	Debit $	Credit $

Ex. 3.26

Happy Nappies
General Ledger
Delivery Vehicle Account

Date	Particulars	Fol	Debit $	Credit $	Balance $

Capital – S Craper Account

Date	Particulars	Fol	Debit $	Credit $	Balance $

Drawings – S Craper Account

Date	Particulars	Fol	Debit $	Credit $	Balance $

Purchases – Chemicals Account

Date	Particulars	Fol	Debit $	Credit $	Balance $

GST Paid Account

Date	Particulars	Fol	Debit $	Credit $	Balance $

Advertising Account

Date	Particulars	Fol	Debit $	Credit $	Balance $

Nappy Cleaning Income Account

Date	Particulars	Fol	Debit $	Credit $	Balance $

Ex. 3.26

Happy Nappies
General Ledger
GST Collected Account

Date	Particulars	Fol	Debit $	Credit $	Balance $

Accounts Receivable Control Account

Date	Particulars	Fol	Debit $	Credit $	Balance $

Accounts Payable Control Account

Date	Particulars	Fol	Debit $	Credit $	Balance $

Delivery Income Account

Date	Particulars	Fol	Debit $	Credit $	Balance $

Washing Machines Account

Date	Particulars	Fol	Debit $	Credit $	Balance $

Washing Machine Repairs Account

Date	Particulars	Fol	Debit $	Credit $	Balance $

Cash at Bank Account

Date	Particulars	Fol	Debit $	Credit $	Balance $

Wages Account

Date	Particulars	Fol	Debit $	Credit $	Balance $

Ex. 3.26

Happy Nappies
General Ledger
Rent Expense Account

Date	Particulars	Fol	Debit $	Credit $	Balance $

Motor Vehicle Repairs Account

Date	Particulars	Fol	Debit $	Credit $	Balance $

Stationery Account

Date	Particulars	Fol	Debit $	Credit $	Balance $

Ex. 3.26

Happy Nappies
Trial Balance as at 30 November 2017

Account name	Debit $	Credit $

Ex. 4.1

B Jackson Retailer
General Ledger
Accounts Receivable Control Account

Date	Particulars	Fol	Debit $	Credit $	Balance $

Accounts Receivable Subsidiary Ledger
1 – B Bartlett Account

Date	Particulars	Fol	Debit $	Credit $	Balance $

2 – C Joseph Account

Date	Particulars	Fol	Debit $	Credit $	Balance $

3 – C Hardwood Account

Date	Particulars	Fol	Debit $	Credit $	Balance $

4 – L Paterson Account

Date	Particulars	Fol	Debit $	Credit $	Balance $

Accounts Receivable Reconciliation Schedule as at 31 July 2017

Account number	Account name	Balance
Total as per Accounts Receivable Control Account		

Ex. 4.2

I Drill, Dentist
General Ledger
Accounts Receivable Control Account

Date	Particulars	Fol	Debit $	Credit $	Balance $
01-Mar-19	Balance				430 Dr
31-Mar-19	Service fees	SJ	1,250		1,680 Dr
	Discount expense	CRJ		4	1,676 Dr
	Cash at bank	CRJ		416	1,260 Dr

Accounts Receivable Subsidiary Ledger
D1 – D Graham Account

Date	Particulars	Fol	Debit $	Credit $	Balance $
01-Mar-19	Balance				250 Dr
31-Mar-19	Cash at bank	CRJ		50	200 Dr

D2 – G Grebio Account

Date	Particulars	Fol	Debit $	Credit $	Balance $

D3 – J Reddrop Account

Date	Particulars	Fol	Debit $	Credit $	Balance $

D4 – American Express Account

Date	Particulars	Fol	Debit $	Credit $	Balance $

D5 – J De Araugo Account

Date	Particulars	Fol	Debit $	Credit $	Balance $

Accounts Receivable Reconciliation Schedule as at 31 March 2019

Account number	Account name	Balance
	Total as per Accounts Receivable Control Account	

Ex. 4.3

B Jackson, Retailer
General Ledger
Accounts Payable Control Account

Date	Particulars	Fol	Debit $	Credit $	Balance $

Accounts Payable Subsidiary Ledger
1 – M Holden Account

Date	Particulars	Fol	Debit $	Credit $	Balance $

2 – A Graham Account

Date	Particulars	Fol	Debit $	Credit $	Balance $

3 – D Senn Account

Date	Particulars	Fol	Debit $	Credit $	Balance $

4 – R Gilchrist Account

Date	Particulars	Fol	Debit $	Credit $	Balance $

5 – T Morrow Account

Date	Particulars	Fol	Debit $	Credit $	Balance $

Accounts Payable Reconciliation Schedule as at 31 July 2017

Account number	Account name	Balance
Total as per Accounts Payable Control Account		

Ex. 4.4

I Drill, Dentist
General Ledger
Accounts Payable Control Account

Date	Particulars	Fol	Debit $	Credit $	Balance $

Accounts Payable Subsidiary Ledger
C1 – N Taig Account

Date	Particulars	Fol	Debit $	Credit $	Balance $

C2 – P Knight Account

Date	Particulars	Fol	Debit $	Credit $	Balance $

C3 – B Boxshall Account

Date	Particulars	Fol	Debit $	Credit $	Balance $

C4 – M Tie Account

Date	Particulars	Fol	Debit $	Credit $	Balance $

C5 – S Bradshaw Account

Date	Particulars	Fol	Debit $	Credit $	Balance $

C6 – D McCaskill Account

Date	Particulars	Fol	Debit $	Credit $	Balance $

Accounts Payable Reconciliation Schedule as at 31 March 2019

Account number	Account name	Balance
	Total as per Accounts Payable Control Account	

Ex. 4.5   **Choo Tran, Retailer**
                                       General Ledger
                          Accounts Receivable Control Account

Date	Particulars	Fol	Debit $	Credit $	Balance $

Accounts Payable Control Account

Date	Particulars	Fol	Debit $	Credit $	Balance $

Accounts Receivable Subsidiary Ledger
D01 – T Larwood Account

Date	Particulars	Fol	Debit $	Credit $	Balance $

D02 – H Ponsford Account

Date	Particulars	Fol	Debit $	Credit $	Balance $

D03 – A Haig Account

Date	Particulars	Fol	Debit $	Credit $	Balance $

Ex. 4.5

Choo Tran, Retailer
D04 – C Wilson Account

Date	Particulars	Fol	Debit $	Credit $	Balance $

D05 – S Reyne Account

Date	Particulars	Fol	Debit $	Credit $	Balance $

D06 – Diners Club Account

Date	Particulars	Fol	Debit $	Credit $	Balance $

Accounts Receivable Reconciliation Schedule as at 31 October 2017

Account number	Account name	Balance
Total as per Accounts Receivable Control Account		

Ex. 4.5

Choo Tran, Retailer
Accounts Payable Subsidiary Ledger
C01 – R McCol Account

Date	Particulars	Fol	Debit $	Credit $	Balance $

C02 – L Hayden Account

Date	Particulars	Fol	Debit $	Credit $	Balance $

C03 – B Hocling Account

Date	Particulars	Fol	Debit $	Credit $	Balance $

C04 – D Brand Account

Date	Particulars	Fol	Debit $	Credit $	Balance $

C05 – F Morris Account

Date	Particulars	Fol	Debit $	Credit $	Balance $

Accounts Payable Reconciliation Schedule as at 31 October 2017

Account number	Account name	Balance
Total as per Accounts Payable Control Account		

Ex. 4.6   Solution in textbook.

J Maxwell, Wholesaler
General Ledger
Accounts Receivable Control Account

Date	Particulars	Fol	Debit $	Credit $	Balance $

Accounts Payable Control Account

Date	Particulars	Fol	Debit $	Credit $	Balance $

Accounts Receivable Subsidiary Ledger
D1 – J Graham Account

Date	Particulars	Fol	Debit $	Credit $	Balance $

D2 – American Express Account

Date	Particulars	Fol	Debit $	Credit $	Balance $

D3 – A Howard Account

Date	Particulars	Fol	Debit $	Credit $	Balance $

Ex. 4.6   Solution in textbook.

J Maxwell, Wholesaler
Accounts Receivable Subsidiary Ledger
D4 – L McDermott Account

Date	Particulars	Fol	Debit $	Credit $	Balance $

D5 – J Enright Account

Date	Particulars	Fol	Debit $	Credit $	Balance $

D6 – L McCrae Account

Date	Particulars	Fol	Debit $	Credit $	Balance $

D7 – M Stacey Account

Date	Particulars	Fol	Debit $	Credit $	Balance $

D8 – M Warne Account

Date	Particulars	Fol	Debit $	Credit $	Balance $

Accounts Receivable Reconciliation Schedule as at 30 June 2019

Account number	Account name	Balance
Total as per Accounts Receivable Control Account		

Ex. 4.6   Solution in textbook.

J Maxwell, Wholesaler
Accounts Payable Subsidiary Ledger
C1 – N Jackson Account

Date	Particulars	Fol	Debit $	Credit $	Balance $

C2 – P Marsh Account

Date	Particulars	Fol	Debit $	Credit $	Balance $

C3 – R Moore Account

Date	Particulars	Fol	Debit $	Credit $	Balance $

C4 – A Blight Account

Date	Particulars	Fol	Debit $	Credit $	Balance $

C5 – A Howard Account

Date	Particulars	Fol	Debit $	Credit $	Balance $

C6 – T Murphy Account

Date	Particulars	Fol	Debit $	Credit $	Balance $

Accounts Payable Reconciliation Schedule as at 30 June 2019

Account number	Account name	Balance
Total as per Accounts Payable Control Account		

Ex. 4.7

Redpath Retailers
General Ledger
Accounts Receivable Control Account

Date	Particulars	Fol	Debit $	Credit $	Balance $

Accounts Payable Control Account

Date	Particulars	Fol	Debit $	Credit $	Balance $

Cash at Bank Account

Date	Particulars	Fol	Debit $	Credit $	Balance $

Stock Account

Date	Particulars	Fol	Debit $	Credit $	Balance $

Furniture and Equipment Account

Date	Particulars	Fol	Debit $	Credit $	Balance $

Motor Vehicles Account

Date	Particulars	Fol	Debit $	Credit $	Balance $

Capital – J Redpath Account

Date	Particulars	Fol	Debit $	Credit $	Balance $

Ex. 4.7

Redpath Retailers
General Ledger
Sales Account

Date	Particulars	Fol	Debit $	Credit $	Balance $

Sales Returns and Allowances Account

Date	Particulars	Fol	Debit $	Credit $	Balance $

Freight Income Account

Date	Particulars	Fol	Debit $	Credit $	Balance $

Purchases Account

Date	Particulars	Fol	Debit $	Credit $	Balance $

Purchases Returns and Allowances Account

Date	Particulars	Fol	Debit $	Credit $	Balance $

Advertising Account

Date	Particulars	Fol	Debit $	Credit $	Balance $

Wages Account

Date	Particulars	Fol	Debit $	Credit $	Balance $

Rent Expense Account

Date	Particulars	Fol	Debit $	Credit $	Balance $

Ex. 4.7

Redpath Retailers
General Ledger
GST Collected Account

Date	Particulars	Fol	Debit $	Credit $	Balance $

GST Paid Account

Date	Particulars	Fol	Debit $	Credit $	Balance $

Land and Buildings Account

Date	Particulars	Fol	Debit $	Credit $	Balance $

Mortgage on Land and Buildings Account

Date	Particulars	Fol	Debit $	Credit $	Balance $

Bad Debts Account

Date	Particulars	Fol	Debit $	Credit $	Balance $

Discount Expense Account

Date	Particulars	Fol	Debit $	Credit $	Balance $

Discount Income Account

Date	Particulars	Fol	Debit $	Credit $	Balance $

Motor Vehicle Expenses Account

Date	Particulars	Fol	Debit $	Credit $	Balance $

Ex. 4.7

Redpath Retailers
Accounts Receivable Subsidiary Ledger
H Milburn Account

Date	Particulars	Fol	Debit $	Credit $	Balance $

P Walters Account

Date	Particulars	Fol	Debit $	Credit $	Balance $

D Chaplin Account

Date	Particulars	Fol	Debit $	Credit $	Balance $

J Chapman Account

Date	Particulars	Fol	Debit $	Credit $	Balance $

Ex. 4.7

Redpath Retailers
Accounts Payable Subsidiary Ledger
R Hutton Account

Date	Particulars	Fol	Debit $	Credit $	Balance $

B Clarke Account

Date	Particulars	Fol	Debit $	Credit $	Balance $

L Haig Account

Date	Particulars	Fol	Debit $	Credit $	Balance $

S Lin Account

Date	Particulars	Fol	Debit $	Credit $	Balance $

Ex. 4.7   **Redpath Retailers**
Trial Balance as at 30 June 2019

Account name	Debit $	Credit $

Accounts Receivable Reconciliation Schedule as at 30 June 2019

Account number	Account name	Balance
Total as per Accounts Receivable Control Account		

Accounts Payable Reconciliation Schedule as at 30 June 2019

Account number	Account name	Balance
Total as per Accounts Payable Control Account		

Ex. 4.8 (a)

Eaglehawk Enterprises
General Ledger
Stock Account

Date	Particulars	Fol	Debit $	Credit $	Balance $

Cash at Bank Account

Date	Particulars	Fol	Debit $	Credit $	Balance $

Premises Account

Date	Particulars	Fol	Debit $	Credit $	Balance $

Furniture and Fittings Account

Date	Particulars	Fol	Debit $	Credit $	Balance $

Motor Vehicle Account

Date	Particulars	Fol	Debit $	Credit $	Balance $

Motor Vehicle Expenses Account

Date	Particulars	Fol	Debit $	Credit $	Balance $

Mortgage on Premises Account

Date	Particulars	Fol	Debit $	Credit $	Balance $

Loan from R Goscinny Account

Date	Particulars	Fol	Debit $	Credit $	Balance $

Capital – G Uderzo Account

Date	Particulars	Fol	Debit $	Credit $	Balance $

Office Equipment Account

Date	Particulars	Fol	Debit $	Credit $	Balance $

Ex. 4.8

Eaglehawk Enterprises
General Ledger
GST Paid Account

Date	Particulars	Fol	Debit $	Credit $	Balance $

Drawings – G Uderzo Account

Date	Particulars	Fol	Debit $	Credit $	Balance $

Purchases Account

Date	Particulars	Fol	Debit $	Credit $	Balance $

Accounts Receivable Control Account

Date	Particulars	Fol	Debit $	Credit $	Balance $

Ex. 4.8

Eaglehawk Enterprises
General Ledger
GST Collected Account

Date	Particulars	Fol	Debit $	Credit $	Balance $

Discount Expense Account

Date	Particulars	Fol	Debit $	Credit $	Balance $

Sales Account

Date	Particulars	Fol	Debit $	Credit $	Balance $

Commission Income Account

Date	Particulars	Fol	Debit $	Credit $	Balance $

Accounts Payable Control Account

Date	Particulars	Fol	Debit $	Credit $	Balance $

Discount Income Account

Date	Particulars	Fol	Debit $	Credit $	Balance $

Wages Account

Date	Particulars	Fol	Debit $	Credit $	Balance $

Ex. 4.8

Eaglehawk Enterprises
General Ledger
Merchant Fees Account

Date	Particulars	Fol	Debit $	Credit $	Balance $

Stationery Account

Date	Particulars	Fol	Debit $	Credit $	Balance $

Advertising Account

Date	Particulars	Fol	Debit $	Credit $	Balance $

Insurance Account

Date	Particulars	Fol	Debit $	Credit $	Balance $

Sales Returns and Allowances Account

Date	Particulars	Fol	Debit $	Credit $	Balance $

Purchases Returns and Allowances Account

Date	Particulars	Fol	Debit $	Credit $	Balance $

Bad Debts Account

Date	Particulars	Fol	Debit $	Credit $	Balance $

Ex. 4.8 (b)

Eaglehawk Enterprises
Accounts Receivable Subsidiary Ledger
M Murphy Account

Date	Particulars	Fol	Debit $	Credit $	Balance $

B Green Account

Date	Particulars	Fol	Debit $	Credit $	Balance $

E Carson Account

Date	Particulars	Fol	Debit $	Credit $	Balance $

Diners Club Account

Date	Particulars	Fol	Debit $	Credit $	Balance $

R Rosen Account

Date	Particulars	Fol	Debit $	Credit $	Balance $

Ex. 4.8 (b)

Eaglehawk Enterprises
Accounts Payable Subsidiary Ledger
B Mitchell Account

Date	Particulars	Fol	Debit $	Credit $	Balance $

L Grant Account

Date	Particulars	Fol	Debit $	Credit $	Balance $

P Corelli Account

Date	Particulars	Fol	Debit $	Credit $	Balance $

G Selton Account

Date	Particulars	Fol	Debit $	Credit $	Balance $

Ex. 4.8

Eaglehawk Enterprises
Trial Balance as at 30 June 2019

Account name	Debit $	Credit $

Accounts Receivable Reconciliation Schedule as at 30 June 2019

Account number	Account name	Balance
Total as per Accounts Receivable Control Account		

Accounts Payable Reconciliation Schedule as at 30 June 2019

Account number	Account name	Balance
Total as per Accounts Payable Control Account		

Ex. 4.9 (a)

Ye Olde Antiques
General Ledger
Advertising Account

Date	Particulars	Fol	Debit $	Credit $	Balance $

Capital – J Morton Account

Date	Particulars	Fol	Debit $	Credit $	Balance $

Cash at Bank Account

Date	Particulars	Fol	Debit $	Credit $	Balance $

Interest Income Account

Date	Particulars	Fol	Debit $	Credit $	Balance $

Commission Expense Account

Date	Particulars	Fol	Debit $	Credit $	Balance $

Accounts Payable Control Account

Date	Particulars	Fol	Debit $	Credit $	Balance $

Accounts Receivable Control Account

Date	Particulars	Fol	Debit $	Credit $	Balance $

Ex. 4.9 (a)

Ye Olde Antiques
General Ledger
Discount Expense Account

Date	Particulars	Fol	Debit $	Credit $	Balance $

Discount Income Account

Date	Particulars	Fol	Debit $	Credit $	Balance $

Furniture and Fittings Account

Date	Particulars	Fol	Debit $	Credit $	Balance $

Land and Buildings Account

Date	Particulars	Fol	Debit $	Credit $	Balance $

Mortgage Loan on Land and Buildings Account

Date	Particulars	Fol	Debit $	Credit $	Balance $

Motor Vehicles Account

Date	Particulars	Fol	Debit $	Credit $	Balance $

Purchases Account

Date	Particulars	Fol	Debit $	Credit $	Balance $

Purchase Returns and Allowances Account

Date	Particulars	Fol	Debit $	Credit $	Balance $

Ex. 4.9 (a)

Ye Olde Antiques
General Ledger
Commission Income Account

Date	Particulars	Fol	Debit $	Credit $	Balance $

Loan from J Morton Account

Date	Particulars	Fol	Debit $	Credit $	Balance $

Sales Account

Date	Particulars	Fol	Debit $	Credit $	Balance $

Motor Vehicle Expenses Account

Date	Particulars	Fol	Debit $	Credit $	Balance $

Sales Returns and Allowances Account

Date	Particulars	Fol	Debit $	Credit $	Balance $

Cartage Inwards Account

Date	Particulars	Fol	Debit $	Credit $	Balance $

Stock Account

Date	Particulars	Fol	Debit $	Credit $	Balance $

Rent Account

Date	Particulars	Fol	Debit $	Credit $	Balance $

Wages Account

Date	Particulars	Fol	Debit $	Credit $	Balance $

Ex. 4.9 (a)

Ye Olde Antiques
General Ledger
Repair Income Account

Date	Particulars	Fol	Debit $	Credit $	Balance $

Bad Debts Account

Date	Particulars	Fol	Debit $	Credit $	Balance $

Telephone Account

Date	Particulars	Fol	Debit $	Credit $	Balance $

GST Collected Account

Date	Particulars	Fol	Debit $	Credit $	Balance $

GST Paid Account

Date	Particulars	Fol	Debit $	Credit $	Balance $

Drawings – J Morton Account

Date	Particulars	Fol	Debit $	Credit $	Balance $

Late Fees Income Account

Date	Particulars	Fol	Debit $	Credit $	Balance $

Ex. 4.9 (b)

Ye Olde Antiques
Accounts Receivable Subsidiary Ledger
Sandberg Servies Co Account

Date	Particulars	Fol	Debit $	Credit $	Balance $

Jon's Distributors Account

Date	Particulars	Fol	Debit $	Credit $	Balance $

Millie's Imports Account

Date	Particulars	Fol	Debit $	Credit $	Balance $

Heritage Warehouse Account

Date	Particulars	Fol	Debit $	Credit $	Balance $

Ex. 4.9 (b)

Ye Olde Antiques
Accounts Payable Subsidiary Ledger
Fine Furnishings Pty Ltd Account

Date	Particulars	Fol	Debit $	Credit $	Balance $

Marti & Co Account

Date	Particulars	Fol	Debit $	Credit $	Balance $

Geneva Fittings Ltd Account

Date	Particulars	Fol	Debit $	Credit $	Balance $

Villikins & Sons Account

Date	Particulars	Fol	Debit $	Credit $	Balance $

Ex. 4.9 (c, d and e)

Ye Olde Antiques
Trial Balance as at 30 November 2019

Account name	Debit $	Credit $

Accounts Receivable Reconciliation Schedule as at 30 November 2019

Account number	Account name	Balance
Total as per Accounts Receivable Control Account		

Accounts Payable Reconciliation Schedule as at 30 November 2019

Account number	Account name	Balance
Total as per Accounts Payable Control Account		

Ex. 4.9

Ye Olde Antiques
Chart of Accounts

Ex. 4.10
(a) Briefly explain the importance of the development of credit policies and procedures.

_____

_____

_____

(b) Briefly outline areas covered by an organisation's credit policy.

_____

_____

_____

_____

_____

_____

Ex. 4.11   Briefly explain the importance of customer credit approval.

_____

_____

_____

Ex. 4.12   Five internal control measures that should exist in the processing of sales invoices.

_____

_____

_____

_____

_____

_____

_____

_____

_____

_____

_____

_____

_____

_____

_____

_____

Ex. 4.13 Outline the internal control benefits of issuing statements to customers.

_____

_____

_____

_____

Ex. 4.14
(a) Nature and content of the report prepared to determine debtors with overdue amounts.

_____

_____

_____

_____

(b) Action taken to facilitate prompt payment of amounts overdue.

_____

_____

_____

_____

_____

_____

_____

_____

Ex. 4.15 Briefly comment on the early identification of doubtful debts.

_____

_____

_____

Ex. 4.16

_____

_____

_____

_____

_____

_____

_____

_____

Ex. 4.17

(a)   Internal controls over the receipt of goods from suppliers.

_____

_____

_____

_____

_____

_____

_____

_____

_____

_____

_____

_____

_____

_____

_____

_____

_____

(b)   Internal controls over the processing of supplier invoices.

_____

_____

_____

_____

_____

_____

_____

_____

_____

_____

_____

_____

_____

_____

_____

_____

_____

_____

_____

_____

Ex. 4.18   Briefly explain the importance of monitoring accounts payable.

_____

_____

_____

_____

_____

_____

_____

_____

Ex. 4.19   Comment briefly on the control over business credit cards.

_____

_____

_____

_____

_____

_____

_____

_____

_____

_____

_____

_____

_____

_____

_____

_____

Ex. 4.20 Briefly explain the concept of reasonableness checks.

Reasonableness checks involve periodic perusal of accounting records by someone in authority,

such as the accountant or financial controller. The aim is to highlight any transactions that appear

out of the ordinary in terms of nature or amount. Any such items should be investigated and

approriate action taken.

_____

_____

_____

_____

_____

Ex. 5.1   **Explain the following:**

(a)   **bank reconciliation statement**

_____

_____

(b)   **bank overdraft**

_____

_____

(c)   **bank fees**

_____

_____

(d)   **bank statement**

_____

_____

Ex. 5.2   **Explain how a cheque account is operated.**

_____

_____

_____

_____

_____

_____

_____

_____

_____

_____

_____

_____

_____

_____

_____

_____

_____

_____

_____

Ex. 5.3   **Three examples each of deposits and withdrawals.**

(a)   **deposits**

_____

(b)   **withdrawals**

_____

Ex. 5.4   **Explain a bank's treatment of an account balance.**

_____

_____

_____

Ex. 5.5

P Parker
Cash Receipts Journal

Date	Particulars	Fol	Ref	Discount expense			Accounts receivable control	Cash sales	Sundries		GST collected	Bank
				Accounts receivable control	GST collected	Discount expense			Amount	Account		
30-Jun-17	Subtotal to date			11	1	10	299	3,500	400		350	4,549

Ex. 5.5

P Parker
Cash Payments Journal

Date	Particulars	Fol	Ref	Discount income			Accounts payable control	Cash purchases	Wages	Sundries		GST paid	Bank
				Accounts payable control	GST paid	Discount income				Amount	Account		
30-Jun-17	Subtotal to date			33	3	30	377	140	300	380		22	1,219

Ex. 5.5

P Parker
General Ledger
Cash at Bank Account

Date	Particulars	Fol	Debit $	Credit $	Balance $

Ex. 5.6   Solution in textbook.

Con Constable
Cash Receipts Journal

Date	Particulars	Fol	Ref	Discount expense			Accounts receivable control	Cash sales	Sundries		GST collected	Bank
				Accounts receivable control	GST collected	Discount expense			Amount	Account		
30-Nov-19	Subtotal to date			33	3	30	270	1,290	200		139	1,899

Ex. 5.6

Con Constable
Cash Payments Journal

Date	Particulars	Fol	Ref	Discount income			Accounts payable control	Cash purchases	Wages	Sundries		GST paid	Bank
				Accounts payable control	GST paid	Discount income				Amount	Account		
30-Nov-19	Subtotal to date			22	2	20	175	300	300	350		40	1,165

Ex. 5.6

Con Constable
General Ledger
Cash at Bank Account

Date	Particulars	Fol	Debit $	Credit $	Balance $

Ex. 5.7 Briefly explain the following:

(a) Deposits not credited

_____

_____

_____

Unpresented cheques

_____

_____

_____

(b) Explain the treatment of these in D U Werk's bank reconcoliation statement.

_____

_____

_____

_____

_____

Ex. 5.8

B Wallace

Cash Receipts Journal (simplified)

Date	Particulars	Ref	Amount	GST Collected	Bank

Ex. 5.8

B Wallace

Cash Payments Journal (simplified)

Date	Particulars	Ref	Amount	GST Paid	Bank

Ex. 5.8

B Wallace
General Ledger
Cash at Bank Account

Date	Particulars	Fol	Debit $	Credit $	Balance $

Ex. 5.8

Bank Reconciliation Statement as at 31 July 2019

Ex. 5.9   Explain C U Later's bank reconciliation statement.

_____

_____

_____

_____

_____

_____

Ex. 5.10   Solution in textbook.

A Mark
Cash Receipts Journal (simplified)

Date	Particulars	Ref	Amount	GST Collected	Bank

Ex. 5.10   **A Mark**
Cash Payments Journal (simplified)

Date	Particulars	Ref	Amount	GST Paid	Bank

Ex. 5.10   Solution in textbook.

A Mark
General Ledger
Cash at Bank Account

Date	Particulars	Fol	Debit $	Credit $	Balance $

Ex. 5.10

A Mark
Bank Reconciliation Statement as at 31 August 2019

_____

_____
_____
_____
_____
_____
_____
_____
_____
_____
_____
_____
_____
_____
_____
_____
_____
_____
_____
_____
_____
_____
_____
_____
_____

Ex. 5.11 (a)

D Dimasi
Cash Receipts Journal (simplified)

Date	Particulars	Ref	Amount	GST Collected	Bank
30-Jun-18	Subtotal to date		1,007.27	42.73	1,050.00

D Dimasi
Cash Payments Journal (simplified)

Date	Particulars	Ref	Amount	GST Paid	Bank
30-Jun-18	Subtotal to date		449.09	30.91	480.00

Ex. 5.11 (b)

D Dimasi
General Ledger
Cash at Bank Account (Asset)

Date	Particulars	Debit $	Credit $	Balance $
31-May-18	Balance			5,000.00 Cr

Ex. 5.11 (c)

D Dimasi
Bank Reconciliation Statement as at 30 June 2018

_____

_____

_____

_____

_____

_____

_____

_____

_____

_____

_____

_____

_____

_____

_____

_____

_____

Ex. 5.12 (a)

B Panchez
Cash Receipts Journal (simplified)

Date	Particulars	Ref	Amount	GST Collected	Bank
31-May-19	Subtotal to date		3,450.18	199.82	3,650.00

B Panchez
Cash Payments Journal (simplified)

Date	Particulars	Ref	Amount	GST Paid	Bank
31-May-19	Subtotal to date		501.83	43.17	545.00

Ex. 5.12 (b)

B Panchez
General Ledger
Cash at Bank Account (Asset)

Date	Particulars	Debit $	Credit $	Balance $

Ex. 5.12 (c)

B Panchez
Bank Reconciliation Statement as at 31 May 2019

Ex. 5.13

E Singh
Cash Receipts Journal

Date	Particulars	Fol	Ref	Discount expense			Accounts receivable control	Cash sales	Sundries		GST collected	Bank
				Accounts receivable control	GST collected	Discount expense			Amount	Account		
31-May-17	Subtotal to date			9.34	0.85	8.49	310.38	128.24			12.82	451.44

Ex. 5.13

E Singh
Cash Payments Journal

Date	Particulars	Fol	Ref	Discount income			Accounts payable control	Cash purchases	Wages	Sundries		GST paid	Bank
				Accounts payable control	GST paid	Discount income				Amount	Account		
31-May-17	Subtotal to date			25.08	2.28	22.80	1,007.70		495.54	3.82		0.38	1,507.44

Ex. 5.13

E Singh
General Ledger
Cash at Bank Account

Date	Particulars	Fol	Debit $	Credit $	Balance $

Ex. 5.13

E Singh
Bank Reconciliation Statement as at 31 May 2017

Ex. 5.14 (a) Solution in textbook.

A Bugg
Cash Receipts Journal

Date	Particulars	Fol	Ref	Discount expense			Accounts receivable control	Cash sales	Sundries		GST collected	Bank
				Accounts receivable control	GST collected	Discount expense			Amount	Account		
31-Aug-19	Subtotal to date			130.00	11.73	118.27	1,410.00	1,323.63			132.37	2,866.00

Ex. 5.14 (a)

A Bugg
Cash Payments Journal

Date	Particulars	Fol	Ref	Discount income			Accounts payable control	Cash purchases	Wages	Sundries		GST paid	Bank
				Accounts payable control	GST paid	Discount income				Amount	Account		
31-Aug-19	Subtotal to date			32.60	2.96	29.64	1,271.40	87.56	2,120.00	955.31		104.29	4,538.56

Exercise 5.14

Ex. 5.14 (b)   Solution in textbook.

A Bugg
General Ledger
Cash at Bank Account

Date	Particulars	Fol	Debit $	Credit $	Balance $

Ex. 5.14 (c)

A Bugg
Bank Reconciliation Statement as at 31 August 2019

Ex. 5.15

B Date
Cash Receipts Journal

Date	Particulars	Fol	Ref	Discount expense			Accounts receivable control	Cash sales	Sundries		GST collected	Bank
				Accounts receiavble control	GST collected	Discount expense			Amount	Account		
30-Nov-19	Subtotal to date			22.00	2.00	20.00	1,587.00	381.82	243.00		38.18	2,250.00

Ex. 5.15

B Date
Cash Payments Journal

Date	Particulars	Fol	Ref	Discount income			Accounts payable control	Cash purchases	Wages	Sundries		GST paid	Bank
				Accounts payable control	GST paid	Discount income				Amount	Account		
30-Nov-19	Subtotal to date			33.00	3.00	30.00	670.00	345.46	70.00	210.00		34.54	1,330.00

Exercise 5.15

Ex. 5.15

B Date
General Ledger
Cash at Bank Account

Date	Particulars	Fol	Debit $	Credit $	Balance $

Ex. 5.15

B Date
Bank Reconciliation Statement as at 30 November 2019

Ex. 5.16 (a)

D Kickett
Cash Receipts Journal

Date	Particulars	Fol	Ref	Discount expense			Cash	Sundries		Accounts receivable control	GST collected	Bank
				Accounts receivable control	GST collected	Discount expense	sales	Amount	Account			
31-Mar-19	Subtotal to date			50.00	4.55	45.45	181.82	90.91		1,400.00	27.27	1,700.00

Ex. 5.16 (a)

D Kickett
Cash Payments Journal

Date	Particulars	Fol	Ref	Discount income			Cash	Accounts payable control	Wages	Sundries		GST paid	Bank
				Accounts payable control	GST paid	Discount income	purchases			Amount	Acount		
31-Mar-19	Subtotal to date			10.00	0.91	9.09	272.73	420.00				27.27	720.00

Ex. 5.16 (b)

D Kickett
General Ledger
Cash at Bank Account

Date	Particulars	Fol	Debit $	Credit $	Balance $

Ex. 5.16 (c)

D Kickett
Bank Reconciliation Statement as at 31 March 2019

Ex. 5.17   Solution in textbook.

B Purchest
Cash Receipts Journal

Date	Particulars	Fol	Ref	Discount expense			Cash	Accounts	Sundries		GST	Bank
				Accounts receivable control	GST collected	Discount expense	sales	receivable control	Amount	Account	collected	
30-Apr-19	Subtotal to date			10.00	0.91	9.09	3,590.91	460.00			359.09	4,410.00

Ex. 5.17

B Purchest
Cash Payments Journal

Date	Particulars	Fol	Ref	Discount income			Cash	Accounts	Wages	Sundries		GST	Bank
				Accounts payable control	GST Paid	Discount income	purchases	payable control		Amount	Account	paid	
30-Apr-19	Subtotal to date			14.00	1.27	12.73	277.27	486.00	85.00	87.27		36.46	972.00

Exercise 5.17

Ex. 5.17   Solution in textbook.

B Purchest
General Ledger
Cash at Bank Account (Asset)

Date	Particulars	Debit $	Credit $	Balance $

Ex. 5.17

B Purchest
Bank Reconciliation Statement as at 30 April 2019

_____

_____

_____

_____

_____

_____

_____

_____

_____

_____

_____

_____

_____

_____

_____

_____

_____

_____

_____

_____

Ex. 5.18 How the cash register or POS device provides internal control over cash receipts.

_____

_____

_____

_____

_____

_____

_____

Ex. 5.19 How a business verifies that EFTPOS and credit card sales have been correctly credited by the bank.

_____

_____

Ex. 5.20 One security measure in relation to banking of cash receipts.

_____

_____

_____

_____

_____

_____

_____

_____

_____

_____

Ex. 5.21 Briefly explain internal control measures for EFT payments.

_____

_____

_____

_____

_____

_____

_____

_____

_____

_____

_____

_____

Ex. 6.1   **Explain petty cash.**

_____

_____

_____

Ex. 6.2   **Why is it important for some businesses to have a petty cash fund?**

_____

_____

_____

Ex. 6.3   **Explain the petty cash imprest system.**

_____

_____

_____

_____

_____

_____

_____

Ex. 6.4   **Explain why petty cash advance is an asset.**

_____

_____

_____

Ex. 6.5   **Explain why the Petty Cash Advance Account is not debited.**

_____

_____

_____

Ex. 6.6   **Factors to consider when appointing a petty cashier.**

_____

_____

_____

Ex. 6.7   E Macquire

Date 2/6/17   No 1
Petty Cash Voucher
Paid to   ...   .
For ....
Amount (inc. GST) $ _____
GST $ _____
Acc no   .
Signed

Date 5/6/17   No 2
Petty Cash Voucher
Paid to   ...   .
For ....
Amount (inc. GST) $ _____
GST $ _____
Acc no   .
Signed

Date 5/6/17   No 3
Petty Cash Voucher
Paid to   ...   .
For ....
Amount (inc. GST) $ _____
GST $ _____
Acc no   .
Signed

Date 12/6/17   No 4
Petty Cash Voucher
Paid to   ...   .
For ....
Amount (inc. GST) $ _____
GST $ _____
Acc no   .
Signed

Date 17/6/17   No 5
Petty Cash Voucher
Paid to   ...   .
For ....
Amount (inc. GST) $ _____
GST $ _____
Acc no   .
Signed

Date 18/6/17   No 6
Petty Cash Voucher
Paid to   ...   .
For ....
Amount (inc. GST) $ _____
GST $ _____
Acc no   .
Signed

Date 26/6/17   No 7
Petty Cash Voucher
Paid to   ...   .
For ....
Amount (inc. GST) $ _____
GST $ _____
Acc no   .
Signed

Date 27/6/17   No 8
Petty Cash Voucher
Paid to   ...   .
For ....
Amount (inc. GST) $ _____
GST $ _____
Acc no   .
Signed

Date 30/6/17   No 9
Petty Cash Voucher
Paid to   ...   .
For ....
Amount (inc. GST) $ _____
GST $ _____
Acc no   .
Signed

Date 30/6/17   No 10
Petty Cash Voucher
Paid to   ...   .
For ....
Amount (inc. GST) $ _____
GST $ _____
Acc no   .
Signed

Ex. 6.8

C Constable
Petty Cash Book

Date	Particulars	Voucher number	Amount received	Petty cash amount	Postage	Travel	Freight	Coffee, tea, etc.	Sundries		GST paid
									Amount	Account	

Exercise 6.8

To Trial Balance Workbook 6e

Ex. 6.9 Solution in textbook.

G Wanganeen
Petty Cash Book

Date	Particulars	Voucher number	Amount received	Petty cash amount	Postage	Travel	Newspapers	Sundries		GST paid
								Amount	Account	

Exercise 6.9

Ex. 6.10

N Schmidt
Petty Cash Book

Date	Particulars	Voucher number	Amount received	Petty cash amount	Postage 416	Travel 418	Coffee, tea, etc. 403	Stationery 419	Sundries Amount	Sundries Account	GST paid 103

Cash Payments Journal (Extract)

Date	Particulars	Fol	Ref	Discount income Accounts payable control	Discount income GST paid	Discount income	Accounts payable control	Cash purchases	Wages	Sundries Amount	Sundries Account	GST paid	Bank

Exercise 6.10

Ex. 6.11 Solution in textbook.

B Minotta
Petty Cash Book

Date	Particulars	Voucher number	Amount received	Petty cash amount	Postage	Travel	News-papers	Sundries		GST paid
								Amount	Account	

B Minotta
Cash Payments Journal (Extract)

Date	Particulars	Fol	Ref	Discount income			Accounts payable control	Cash purchases	Wages	Sundries		GST paid	Bank
				Accounts payable control	GST paid	Discount income				Amount	Account		

Ex. 6.11 Solution in textbook.

B Minotta
General Ledger
102 – Petty Cash Advance Account

Date	Particulars	Fol	Debit $	Credit $	Balance $

416 – Postage Account

Date	Particulars	Fol	Debit $	Credit $	Balance $

418 – Travel Account

Date	Particulars	Fol	Debit $	Credit $	Balance $

403 – Coffee/Tea Account

Date	Particulars	Fol	Debit $	Credit $	Balance $

410 – Donations Account

Date	Particulars	Fol	Debit $	Credit $	Balance $

419 – Stationery Account

Date	Particulars	Fol	Debit $	Credit $	Balance $

422 – Newspapers Account

Date	Particulars	Fol	Debit $	Credit $	Balance $

450 – Cash Under/Over Account

Date	Particulars	Fol	Debit $	Credit $	Balance $

101 – Cash at Bank Account

Date	Particulars	Fol	Debit $	Credit $	Balance $

103 – GST Paid Account

Date	Particulars	Fol	Debit $	Credit $	Balance $

To Trial Balance Workbook 6e

Ex. 6.12 (a)

T Bright
Petty Cash Book

Date	Particulars	Voucher number	Amount received	Petty cash amount	Postage 416	Travel 418	Stationery 402	Sundries Amount	Sundries Acc No.	GST paid 207

Exercise 6.12

Ex. 6.12 (b–d)

No. 000634	Commonwealth Bank	No. 000634
Date _____		Stamp duty paid
To _____		
For _____		Date _____
	Pay _____ or bearer	
	The sum of _____	$ _____
Balance		
Deposits		
This cheque		
Balance		

T Bright
Cash Payments Journal (Extract)

Date	Particulars	Fol	Ref	Discount income			Accounts payable control	Cash purchases	Wages	Sundries		GST paid	Bank
				Accounts payable control	GST paid	Discount Income				Amount	Account		

Ex. 6.12

T Bright
General Ledger
102 – Petty Cash Advance Account

Date	Particulars	Fol	Debit $	Credit $	Balance $

416 – Postage Account

Date	Particulars	Fol	Debit $	Credit $	Balance $

418 – Travel Account

Date	Particulars	Fol	Debit $	Credit $	Balance $

402 – Stationery Account

Date	Particulars	Fol	Debit $	Credit $	Balance $

422 – Sundry Expenses Account

Date	Particulars	Fol	Debit $	Credit $	Balance $

101 – Cash at Bank Account

Date	Particulars	Fol	Debit $	Credit $	Balance $

107 – GST Paid Account

Date	Particulars	Fol	Debit $	Credit $	Balance $

Ex. 6.13 (a–c)

J Peart
Petty Cash Book

Date	Particulars	Voucher number	Amount received	Petty cash amount	Postage	Stationery	Travel	Sundries		GST paid
								Amount	Account	

J Peart
Cash Payments Journal (Extract)

Date	Particulars	Fol	Ref	Accounts payable control	Discount income	GST paid	Accounts payable control	Cash purchases	Wages	Sundries		GST paid	Bank
										Amount	Account		

Exercise 6.13

Ex. 6.13 (d)   **J Peart**
                              General Ledger
                        Petty Cash Advance Account

Date	Particulars	Fol	Debit $	Credit $	Balance $

Postage Account

Date	Particulars	Fol	Debit $	Credit $	Balance $

Stationery Account

Date	Particulars	Fol	Debit $	Credit $	Balance $

Travel Account

Date	Particulars	Fol	Debit $	Credit $	Balance $

Misc Expenses Account

Date	Particulars	Fol	Debit $	Credit $	Balance $

GST Paid Account

Date	Particulars	Fol	Debit $	Credit $	Balance $

Cash Under/Over Account

Date	Particulars	Fol	Debit $	Credit $	Balance $

Cash at Bank Account

Date	Particulars	Fol	Debit $	Credit $	Balance $

Ex. 6.14

C Roc
General Ledger
Accounts Payable Control Account

Date	Particulars	Fol	Debit $	Credit $	Balance $

GST Paid Account

Date	Particulars	Fol	Debit $	Credit $	Balance $

Discount Income Account

Date	Particulars	Fol	Debit $	Credit $	Balance $

Purchases Account

Date	Particulars	Fol	Debit $	Credit $	Balance $

Wages Account

Date	Particulars	Fol	Debit $	Credit $	Balance $

Petty Cash Advance Account

Date	Particulars	Fol	Debit $	Credit $	Balance $

Rent Expense Account

Date	Particulars	Fol	Debit $	Credit $	Balance $

Postage Account

Date	Particulars	Fol	Debit $	Credit $	Balance $

Stationery Account

Date	Particulars	Fol	Debit $	Credit $	Balance $

Ex. 6.14

C Roc
General Ledger
Travel Account

Date	Particulars	Fol	Debit $	Credit $	Balance $

Misc Expenses Account

Date	Particulars	Fol	Debit $	Credit $	Balance $

Cash at Bank Account

Date	Particulars	Fol	Debit $	Credit $	Balance $

Ex. 6.15   Briefly outline control procedures for recording petty cash transactions.

_____
_____
_____
_____
_____
_____
_____
_____
_____
_____
_____
_____
_____
_____
_____
_____
_____
_____
_____
_____
_____
_____

Ex. 6.16   How does the imprest system assist in internal control over petty cash?

_____
_____
_____
_____
_____

Ex. 7.1   **Distinguish between:**

(a) **To whom should enquiry be directed?**

_____

_____

(b) **Sections or departments of the business likely to resolve the enquiry.**

_____

_____

_____

_____

Ex. 7.2   **Discuss the objectives of a system of control over payroll.**

_____

_____

_____

_____

_____

_____

_____

_____

_____

Ex. 7.3   **Typical internal control measures of a payroll system.**

_____

_____

_____

_____

_____

_____

_____

_____

_____

_____

_____

_____

_____

Ex. 7.4   **Discuss records that need to be kept for each employee.**

_____

_____

_____

_____

Ex. 7.5   **Discuss the differences between:**

 An award

_____

_____

 An enterprise agreement

_____

_____

_____

Ex. 7.6

_____
_____
_____
_____
_____

Ex. 7.7
Solution in textbook.

_____
_____
_____
_____
_____
_____
_____
_____

Ex. 7.8

_____
_____
_____
_____

Ex. 7.9
Solution in textbook.

_____
_____
_____
_____
_____

Ex. 7.10

_____

Ex. 7.11

_____

Ex. 7.12

_____

Ex. 7.13

_____

_____

_____

_____

_____

Ex. 7.14

_____

_____

_____

_____

Ex. 7.15

_____

_____

_____

Ex. 7.16

Solution in textbook.

_____

_____

_____

_____

_____

Ex. 7.17

_____

_____

_____

Ex. 7.18

_____

_____

_____

Ex. 7.19

_____
_____
_____
_____
_____
_____
_____
_____
_____
_____
_____
_____
_____
_____
_____
_____
_____

Ex. 7.20

_____
_____
_____
_____
_____
_____
_____
_____
_____
_____
_____
_____
_____
_____
_____

Ex. 7.21
Solution in textbook.

_____
_____
_____
_____
_____
_____

Ex. 7.22

Outback Caravan Sales
Payroll register for week ending 6 September 2017

| Employee | Gross earnings | | | | Deductions | | | | Net pay |
	Ord	O'time	Other	Total	Tax	Super	Union	Total	

Ex. 7.22

Outback Caravan Sales
Payroll register for week ending 13 September 2017

| Employee | Gross earnings | | | | Deductions | | | | Net pay |
	Ord	O'time	Other	Total	Tax	Super	Union	Total	

Workings:

Exercise 7.22

Ex. 7.22

Outback Caravan Sales

Payroll register for week ending 20 September 2017

Employee	Gross earnings				Deductions				Net pay
	Ord	O'time	Other	Total	Tax	Super	Union	Total	

Ex. 7.22

Outback Caravan Sales

Payroll register for week ending 27 September 2017

Employee	Gross earnings				Deductions				Net pay
	Ord	O'time	Other	Total	Tax	Super	Union	Total	

Workings:

Exercise 7.22 (2)

Ex. 7.22

Outback Caravan Sales
Employee Earnings Record

Name: Paulene Piper
Address: 23 Brash Street, Mill Park

Employee No: 01

Week Ending	Gross Pay	Deductions				Net pay	Accumulated figures			
		Tax	Super	Union	Other	Total		Gross	Tax	Super	Union

Workings:

To Trial Balance Workbook 6e

Ex. 7.23

Amaroo Office Supplies
Payroll register for week ending 22 November 2019

| Employee | Gross Earnings | | | | Deductions | | | | | Net pay |
	Ord	Annual leave	Other	Total	Tax	Med	Super	Insurance	Total	

Workings

Ex. 7.24   Solution in textbook.

Bright Spark Electrical Services
Payroll register for week ending 30 June 2018

Employee	Gross earnings						Deductions						Net
	Ord	O'time	Annual leave	A/L loading	Other	Total	Tax	Med	Union	Super	Total		pay

Workings

Ex. 7.25

Outback Caravan Sales
General Journal

Date	Particulars	Fol	Debit $	Credit $

Ex. 7.25

Outback Caravan Sales
Cash Payments Journal

Date	Particulars	Fol	Ref	Accounts payable control	Wages	Sundries		GST paid	Bank
						Amount	Account		

Exercise 7.25 (2)

Ex. 7.25   **Outback Caravan Sales**
General Ledger
Superannuation Payable Account

Date	Particulars	Fol	Debit $	Credit $	Balance $

Union Dues Payable Account

Date	Particulars	Fol	Debit $	Credit $	Balance $

Wages Expense Account

Date	Particulars	Fol	Debit $	Credit $	Balance $

PAYG Witholding Payable Account

Date	Particulars	Fol	Debit $	Credit $	Balance $

Wages Payable Account

Date	Particulars	Fol	Debit $	Credit $	Balance $

Bank Account

Date	Particulars	Fol	Debit $	Credit $	Balance $

Ex. 7.26 (a)   **Rex Wholesalers**
                                              General Journal

Date	Particulars	Fol	Debit $	Credit $

To Trial Balance Workbook 6e

Ex. 7.26 (a, b)

Rex Wholesalers
Cash Payments Journal

Date	Particulars	Fol	Ref	Accounts payable control	Wages	Sundries		GST paid	Bank
						Amount	Account		

Exercise 7.26 (2)

Ex. 7.26 (c)
Rex Wholesalers
General Ledger
Wages Expense Account

Date	Particulars	Fol	Debit $	Credit $	Balance $

PAYG Witholding Payable Account

Date	Particulars	Fol	Debit $	Credit $	Balance $

Medical Payable Account

Date	Particulars	Fol	Debit $	Credit $	Balance $

Union Dues Payable Account

Date	Particulars	Fol	Debit $	Credit $	Balance $

Wages Payable Account

Date	Particulars	Fol	Debit $	Credit $	Balance $

Ex.7.26 (a, b)

Rex Wholesalers
General Ledger
Provision for Annual Leave Account

Date	Particulars	Fol	Debit $	Credit $	Balance $

Provision for Long Service Leave Account

Date	Particulars	Fol	Debit $	Credit $	Balance $

Bank Account

Date	Particulars	Fol	Debit $	Credit $	Balance $

Ex. 7.27   **Solution in textbook.**

Laidler Distributors
General Journal

Date	Particulars	Fol	Debit $	Credit $

To Trial Balance Workbook 6e

Ex. 7.27   Solution in textbook.

Laidler Distributors
Cash Payments Journal

Date	Particulars	Ref	Accounts payable control	Wages	Sundries Amount	Sundries Account	GST paid	Bank

Exercise 7.27 (2)

Ex. 7.27 **Solution in Textbook**

Laidler Distributors
General Ledger
Wages Expense Account

Date	Particulars	Fol	Debit $	Credit $	Balance $

PAYG Witholding Payable Account

Date	Particulars	Fol	Debit $	Credit $	Balance $

Superannuation Payable Account

Date	Particulars	Fol	Debit $	Credit $	Balance $

Social Club Payable Account

Date	Particulars	Fol	Debit $	Credit $	Balance $

Union Dues Payable Account

Date	Particulars	Fol	Debit $	Credit $	Balance $

Ex. 7.27   **Solution in textbook.**

Laidler Distributors
General Ledger
Wages Payable Account

Date	Particulars	Fol	Debit $	Credit $	Balance $

Provision for Annual Leave Account

Date	Particulars	Fol	Debit $	Credit $	Balance $

Provision for Long Service Leave Account

Date	Particulars	Fol	Debit $	Credit $	Balance $

Cash at Bank Account

Date	Particulars	Fol	Debit $	Credit $	Balance $

Ex. 7.28   **Workings**

Ex. 7.28 (a)

Richardson and Hafajee, Master Builders

Payroll register for week ending 4 March 2018

| Employee | Gross earnings | | | | Deductions | | | | | Net pay |
	Ord	O'time	Other	Total	Tax	Med	Insurance	Super	Total	

Richardson and Hafajee, Master Builders

Payroll register for week ending 11 March 2018

| Employee | Gross earnings | | | | Deductions | | | | | Net pay |
	Ord	O'time	Other	Total	Tax	Med	Insurance	Super	Total	

Exercise 7.28 (2)

Ex. 7.28 (a)

Richardson and Hafajee, Master Builders
Payroll register for week ending 18 March 2018

| Employee | Gross earnings | | | Deductions | | | | | Net pay |
	Ord	O'time	Other	Total	Tax	Med	Insurance	Super	Total	

Richardson and Hafajee, Master Builders
Payroll register for week ending 25 March 2018

| Employee | Gross earnings | | | Deductions | | | | | Net pay |
	Ord	O'time	Other	Total	Tax	Med	Insurance	Super	Total	

Exercise 7.28 (3)

Ex. 7.28 (b)   **Richardson and Hafajee, Master Builders**
                                            General Journal

Date	Particulars	Fol	Debit $	Credit $

Ex. 7.28 (b)

Richardson and Hafajee, Master Builders
Cash Payments Journal

Date	Particulars	Fol	Ref	Accounts payable control	Wages	Sundries		GST paid	Bank
						Amount	Acccount		

Exercise 7.28 (5)

Ex. 7.28 (c)

Richardson and Hafajee, Master Builders
General Ledger
Wages Expense Account

Date	Particulars	Fol	Debit $	Credit $	Balance $

PAYG Withholding Payable Account

Date	Particulars	Fol	Debit $	Credit $	Balance $

Superannuation Payable Account

Date	Particulars	Fol	Debit $	Credit $	Balance $

Medical Payable Account

Date	Particulars	Fol	Debit $	Credit $	Balance $

Insurance Payable Account

Date	Particulars	Fol	Debit $	Credit $	Balance $

Ex. 7.28 (c)

Richardson and Hafajee, Master Builders
General Ledger
Wages Payable Account

Date	Particulars	Fol	Debit $	Credit $	Balance $

Provision for Annual Leave Account

Date	Particulars	Fol	Debit $	Credit $	Balance $

Provision for Long Service Leave Account

Date	Particulars	Fol	Debit $	Credit $	Balance $

Cash at Bank Account

Date	Particulars	Fol	Debit $	Credit $	Balance $

Ex. 7.28 (d) Year-end responsibilities for employers.

_____
_____
_____
_____
_____
_____
_____
_____
_____
_____
_____
_____
_____
_____
_____
_____

Ex. 7.29

Lane's Plumbing
Payroll register for week ending 7 May 2018

| Employee | Gross earnings | | | | Deductions | | | | | Net pay |
	Ord	O'time	Other	Total	Tax	Med	Super	Union	Total	

Workings

Ex. 7.29

Lane's Plumbing
General Journal

Date	Particulars	Fol	Debit $	Credit $

Ex. 7.29

Lane's Plumbing
Cash Payments Journal

Date	Particulars	Fol	Ref	Accounts payable control	Wages payable	Sundries		GST paid	Bank
						Amount	Account		

Exercise 7.29 (2)

Ex. 7.30 (a) Solution in textbook.

Payroll register

Period ending:

DEPARTMENT

		$		$		$		$		$		$		$		$
Gross Earnings	Ord																
	O'time																
	Travel																
	Adjustments																
	Total																
Deductions	Tax																
	Super																
	Medical																
	Savings																
	Total																
	Net pay																
	Emp'ee no.																

Calculation of tax

_____

_____

_____

_____

_____

_____

_____

_____

Exercise 7.30 (a)

Ex. 7.30 (a)

Calculation of tax (continued)

_____

_____

_____

_____

_____

_____

_____

_____

Ex. 7.30 (b)

Zoe Products

Employee Earnings Record

Name: Employee No: Loaction:

Address: Tax File Number:

Week ending	Gross earnings to date					Tax	Deductions				Net pay
	Ord	O/time	Travel	Adj	Total		Super	Med	Savings	Total	

Exercise 7.30 (a) (2) & (b)

Ex. 7.31

Skidmore Car Sales
General Journal

Date	Particulars	Fol	Debit $	Credit $

Ex. 7.31

Skidmore Car Sales
Cash Payments Journal

Date	Particulars	Ref	Accounts payable control	Wages	Sundries		GST paid	Bank
					Amount	Account		

Exercise 7.31

Ex. 7.31

Skidmore Car Sales
General Ledger
Payroll Tax Expense Account

Date	Particulars	Fol	Debit $	Credit $	Balance $

Payroll Tax Payable Account

Date	Particulars	Fol	Debit $	Credit $	Balance $

Workers' Compensation Expense Account

Date	Particulars	Fol	Debit $	Credit $	Balance $

Workers' Compensation Prepaid Account

Date	Particulars	Fol	Debit $	Credit $	Balance $

Superannuation Expense Account

Date	Particulars	Fol	Debit $	Credit $	Balance $

Superannuation Payable Account

Date	Particulars	Fol	Debit $	Credit $	Balance $

Bank Account

Date	Particulars	Fol	Debit $	Credit $	Balance $

ACCOUNTING
BASIC REPORTS

WORKBOOK

DISK INCLUDED
WITH UWATCH DEMONSTRATIONS
AND ADDITIONAL EXERCISES

Ex. 1.1   Brief outline of the Australian Accounting Standards Board.

_____

_____

_____

Ex. 1.2   Brief description of the Conceptual Framework post convergence with IFRS.

_____

_____

_____

_____

_____

Ex. 1.3   List three users of the financial reports of a business.

_____

_____

Ex. 1.4   Explain the important role of the *Framework for the Preparation and Presentation of Financial Statements* in the context of financial reporting.

Ex. 1.5   Briefly define these items.

(a)   Reporting entity

_____
_____
_____
_____
_____
_____
_____
_____
_____

(b)   GAAP

_____
_____
_____
_____
_____

(c)   General Purpose Financial Report

_____
_____
_____
_____

Ex. 1.6   Briefly explain accounting standards.

_____
_____
_____
_____

Ex. 1.7 Solution in textbook.

(a)   Situations in which it is mandatory to comply with accounting standards

_____
_____
_____
_____

(b)   Situations in which it is mandatory to comply with Statements of Accounting Concepts

_____
_____
_____
_____

Ex. 1.8   The four major financial statements that constitute financial reports.

_____

_____

_____

_____

Ex. 1.9   Briefly describe the nature of the following financial statements.

(a)   Statement of comprehensive income

_____

_____

(b)   Statement of financial position

_____

_____

(c)   Statement of cash flows

_____

_____

Ex. 1.10

Role of statement of comprehensive income in management of the business.

_____

_____

Role of statement of financial position in management of the business.

_____

_____

_____

Ex. 1.11   Briefly describe the nature and purpose of an accounting system.

_____

_____

_____

_____

Ex. 1.12 Factors that influence the design of an accounting system.

_____

_____

_____

_____

_____

_____

_____

Ex. 1.13 Describe the role of the chart of accounts in the design of an accounting system.

_____

_____

_____

_____

Ex. 2.1

(a)   Briefly explain the accounting period convention.

(b)   Briefly explain accrual accounting.

Ex. 2.2

(a)   Briefly explain accrued income.

(b)   Briefly explain accrued expenses.

Ex. 2.3 (a)	C Change				
	General Journal				
Date	Particulars		Fol	Debit $	Credit $

Ex. 2.3 (b)	C Change				
	General Ledger				
	Commission Income Account				
Date	Particulars	Fol	Debit $	Credit $	Balance $

	Interest Income Account				
Date	Particulars	Fol	Debit $	Credit $	Balance $

	GST Collected Account				
Date	Particulars	Fol	Debit $	Credit $	Balance $

	Accrued Income Account				
Date	Particulars	Fol	Debit $	Credit $	Balance $

Ex. 2.4 (a)

C Moore

General Journal

Date	Particulars		Fol	Debit $	Credit $
30-Jun-17	Wages			2,100	
	Interest expense			800	
	Accrued expenses				2,900
	Accrued expenses.				

Ex. 2.4 (b)

C Moore

General Ledger

Wages Account

Date	Particulars	Fol	Debit $	Credit $	Balance $

Interest Expense Account

Date	Particulars	Fol	Debit $	Credit $	Balance $

Accrued Expenses Account

Date	Particulars	Fol	Debit $	Credit $	Balance $

Ex. 2.5 (a)

A Tran
General Journal

Date	Particulars	Fol	Debit $	Credit $

Ex. 2.5 (b)

A Tran
General Ledger
Rent Income

Date	Particulars	Fol	Debit $	Credit $	Balance $

Advertising Account

Date	Particulars	Fol	Debit $	Credit $	Balance $

GST Collected Account

Date	Particulars	Fol	Debit $	Credit $	Balance $

GST Paid Account

Date	Particulars	Fol	Debit $	Credit $	Balance $

Accrued Income Account

Date	Particulars	Fol	Debit $	Credit $	Balance $

Accrued Expenses Account

Date	Particulars	Fol	Debit $	Credit $	Balance $

Ex. 2.6 (a)

L Driver
General Journal

Date	Particulars		Fol	Debit $	Credit $

Ex. 2.6 (b)

L Driver
General Ledger
Annual Leave Expense Account

Date	Particulars	Fol	Debit $	Credit $	Balance $

Provision for Annual Leave Account

Date	Particulars	Fol	Debit $	Credit $	Balance $

Long Service Leave Expense Account

Date	Particulars	Fol	Debit $	Credit $	Balance $

Provision for Long Service Leave Account

Date	Particulars	Fol	Debit $	Credit $	Balance $

Personal Leave Expense Account

Date	Particulars	Fol	Debit $	Credit $	Balance $

Provision for Personal Leave Account

Date	Particulars	Fol	Debit $	Credit $	Balance $

Ex. 2.7 (a)

A Brock
General Journal

Date	Particulars	Fol	Debit $	Credit $

Ex. 2.7 (b)

A Brock
General Ledger
Provision for Annual Leave Account

Date	Particulars	Fol	Debit $	Credit $	Balance $

Provision for Long Service Leave Account

Date	Particulars	Fol	Debit $	Credit $	Balance $

Provision for Personal Leave Account

Date	Particulars	Fol	Debit $	Credit $	Balance $

Annual Leave Expense Account

Date	Particulars	Fol	Debit $	Credit $	Balance $

Long Service Leave Expense Account

Date	Particulars	Fol	Debit $	Credit $	Balance $

Personal Leave Expense Account

Date	Particulars	Fol	Debit $	Credit $	Balance $

Ex. 2.8 (a)				
	S Hafajee			
	General Journal			
Date	Particulars	Fol	Debit $	Credit $

Ex. 2.8 (b)

S Hafajee
General Ledger
Wages Account

Date	Particulars	Fol	Debit $	Credit $	Balance $

Power and Light Account

Date	Particulars	Fol	Debit $	Credit $	Balance $

Commission Income Account

Date	Particulars	Fol	Debit $	Credit $	Balance $

GST Collected Account

Date	Particulars	Fol	Debit $	Credit $	Balance $

GST Paid Account

Date	Particulars	Fol	Debit $	Credit $	Balance $

Annual Leave Expense Account

Date	Particulars	Fol	Debit $	Credit $	Balance $

Provision for Annual Leave Account

Date	Particulars	Fol	Debit $	Credit $	Balance $

Personal Leave Expense Account

Date	Particulars	Fol	Debit $	Credit $	Balance $

Provision for Personal Leave Account

Date	Particulars	Fol	Debit $	Credit $	Balance $

Accrued Expenses Account

Date	Particulars	Fol	Debit $	Credit $	Balance $

Accrued Income Account

Date	Particulars	Fol	Debit $	Credit $	Balance $

Ex. 2.9 (a)	Solution in textbook.			
	J Wilson			
	General Journal			
Date	Particulars	Fol	Debit $	Credit $

Ex. 2.9 (b)	Solution in textbook.				

J Wilson

General Ledger

Loan to M Poustie Account

Date	Particulars	Fol	Debit $	Credit $	Balance $

Interest from M Poustie Account

Date	Particulars	Fol	Debit $	Credit $	Balance $

Wages Account

Date	Particulars	Fol	Debit $	Credit $	Balance $

Provision for Personal Leave Account

Date	Particulars	Fol	Debit $	Credit $	Balance $

Provision for Annual Leave Account

Date	Particulars	Fol	Debit $	Credit $	Balance $

Commission Expense Account

Date	Particulars	Fol	Debit $	Credit $	Balance $

GST Paid Account

Date	Particulars	Fol	Debit $	Credit $	Balance $

Ex. 2.9 (b)   Solution in textbook.

J Wilson
General Ledger
Accrued Income Account

Date	Particulars	Fol	Debit $	Credit $	Balance $

Accrued Expenses Account

Date	Particulars	Fol	Debit $	Credit $	Balance $

Personal Leave Expense Account

Date	Particulars	Fol	Debit $	Credit $	Balance $

Annual Leave Expense Account

Date	Particulars	Fol	Debit $	Credit $	Balance $

Long Service Leave Expense Account

Date	Particulars	Fol	Debit $	Credit $	Balance $

Provision for Long Service Leave Account

Date	Particulars	Fol	Debit $	Credit $	Balance $

Ex. 2.10 (a)	Briefly explain prepaid income.			
Ex. 2.10 (b)	Briefly explain prepaid expenses.			
Ex. 2.11 (a)				

C Change
General Journal

Date	Particulars	Fol	Debit $	Credit $

Ex. 2.11 (b)

C Change
General Ledger

Rent Income Account

Date	Particulars	Fol	Debit $	Credit $	Balance $

Insurance Expense Account

Date	Particulars	Fol	Debit $	Credit $	Balance $

Purchases of Stationery Account

Date	Particulars	Fol	Debit $	Credit $	Balance $

GST Collected Account

Date	Particulars	Fol	Debit $	Credit $	Balance $

GST Paid Account

Date	Particulars	Fol	Debit $	Credit $	Balance $

Prepaid Income Account

Date	Particulars	Fol	Debit $	Credit $	Balance $

Prepaid Expenses Account

Date	Particulars	Fol	Debit $	Credit $	Balance $

Cost of Stationery Used Account

Date	Particulars	Fol	Debit $	Credit $	Balance $

Stock of Stationery on Hand Account

Date	Particulars	Fol	Debit $	Credit $	Balance $

Ex. 2.12 (a)	Solution in textbook.				
	C Constantinou				
	General Journal				
Date	**Particulars**		**Fol**	**Debit $**	**Credit $**

Ex. 2.12 (b)					
	C Constantinou				
	General Ledger				
	Rent Expense Account				
Date	**Particulars**		**Fol**	**Debit $**	**Credit $**	**Balance $**

	Commission Income Account				
Date	**Particulars**		**Fol**	**Debit $**	**Credit $**	**Balance $**

Ex. 2.12 (b)   Solution in textbook.

C Constantinou
General Ledger
Stock of Cleaning Materials Account

Date	Particulars	Fol	Debit $	Credit $	Balance $

Purchases of Cleaning Materials Account

Date	Particulars	Fol	Debit $	Credit $	Balance $

GST Collected Account

Date	Particulars	Fol	Debit $	Credit $	Balance $

GST Paid Account

Date	Particulars	Fol	Debit $	Credit $	Balance $

Prepaid Expenses Account

Date	Particulars	Fol	Debit $	Credit $	Balance $

Prepaid Income Account

Date	Particulars	Fol	Debit $	Credit $	Balance $

Cost of Cleaning Materials Used Account

Date	Particulars	Fol	Debit $	Credit $	Balance $

Ex. 2.13			Debit $	Credit $
	A Ferrier			
	General Journal			
Date	Particulars	Fol		

Ex. 2.14 (a)

L Driver
General Journal

Date	Particulars	Fol	Debit $	Credit $

Ex. 2.14 (b)	L Driver				
	General Ledger				
	Wages Expense Account				
Date	Particulars	Fol	Debit $	Credit $	Balance $

	Rent Income Account				
Date	Particulars	Fol	Debit $	Credit $	Balance $

	Interest Income Account				
Date	Particulars	Fol	Debit $	Credit $	Balance $

	Insurance Account				
Date	Particulars	Fol	Debit $	Credit $	Balance $

	Stock of Stationery on Hand Account				
Date	Particulars	Fol	Debit $	Credit $	Balance $

	Purchases of Stationery Account				
Date	Particulars	Fol	Debit $	Credit $	Balance $

	GST Collected Account				
Date	Particulars	Fol	Debit $	Credit $	Balance $

Ex. 2.14 (b)

L Driver
General Ledger
GST Paid Account

Date	Particulars	Fol	Debit $	Credit $	Balance $

Accrued Expenses Account

Date	Particulars	Fol	Debit $	Credit $	Balance $

Prepaid Income Account

Date	Particulars	Fol	Debit $	Credit $	Balance $

Accrued Income Account

Date	Particulars	Fol	Debit $	Credit $	Balance $

Prepaid Expenses Account

Date	Particulars	Fol	Debit $	Credit $	Balance $

Cost of Stationery Used Account

Date	Particulars	Fol	Debit $	Credit $	Balance $

Ex. 2.15				
	S McKerrow			
	General Journal			
Date	Particulars	Fol	Debit $	Credit $
Ex. 2.16	Importance of analysis of the Accounts Receivable Subsidiary Ledger.			

Ex. 2.17 (a)

L Czarnuch
General Journal

Date	Particulars		Fol	Debit $	Credit $

Ex. 2.17 (b)

L Czarnuch
General Ledger
Accounts Receivable Control Account

Date	Particulars	Fol	Debit $	Credit $	Balance $

Bad Debts Account

Date	Particulars	Fol	Debit $	Credit $	Balance $

GST Collected Account

Date	Particulars	Fol	Debit $	Credit $	Balance $

Allowance for Doubtful Debts Account

Date	Particulars	Fol	Debit $	Credit $	Balance $

Doubtful Debts Account

Date	Particulars	Fol	Debit $	Credit $	Balance $

Ex. 2.17 (c)	Explain the difference between bad and doubtful debts.			
Ex. 2.18	Solution in textbook.			

D McAlpine
General Journal

Date	Particulars	Fol	Debit $	Credit $

Ex. 2.19 (a)				

Wholly Tooth Confectionery Wholesalers
General Journal

Date	Particulars	Fol	Debit $	Credit $

Ex. 2.19 (b)

Wholly Tooth Confectionery Wholesalers
General Ledger
Accumulated Depreciation – Motor Vehicles Account

Date	Particulars	Fol	Debit $	Credit $	Balance $

Accumulated Depreciation – Fixtures and Fittings Account

Date	Particulars	Fol	Debit $	Credit $	Balance $

Depreciation – Motor Vehicles Account

Date	Particulars	Fol	Debit $	Credit $	Balance $

Depreciation – Fixtures and Fittings Account

Date	Particulars	Fol	Debit $	Credit $	Balance $

Ex. 2.20 (a)

Laurie Edger, Public Accountant
General Journal

Date	Particulars	Fol	Debit $	Credit $
Calculations				

Ex. 2.20 (b)

Laurie Edger, Public Accountant
General Ledger
Accumulated Depreciation – Office Equipment Account

Date	Particulars	Fol	Debit $	Credit $	Balance $

Accumulated Depreciation – Motor Vehicle Account

Date	Particulars	Fol	Debit $	Credit $	Balance $

Depreciation – Office Equipment Account

Date	Particulars	Fol	Debit $	Credit $	Balance $

Depreciation – Motor Vehicle Account

Date	Particulars	Fol	Debit $	Credit $	Balance $

Ex. 2.21

Mighty, Clothing Retailer
General Journal

Date	Particulars	Fol	Debit $	Credit $

Ex. 2.22

P Current, Electrical Wholesaler
General Journal

Date	Particulars	Fol	Debit $	Credit $

Ex. 2.23   Solution in textbook.
L Suite, Furniture Retailer

Error 1

(a)
_____

_____

_____

(b)   **General Journal**

Date	Particulars	Fol	Debit $	Credit $

(c)
_____

_____

_____

Error 2

(a)
_____

_____

_____

(b)   **General Journal**

Date	Particulars	Fol	Debit $	Credit $

(c)
_____

_____

_____

Ex. 2.23   Solution in textbook.

Error 3

(a) _____

_____

_____

(b)   **General Journal**

Date	Particulars	Fol	Debit $	Credit $

(c) _____

_____

_____

Error 4

(a) _____

_____

_____

(b)   **General Journal**

Date	Particulars	Fol	Debit $	Credit $

(c) _____

_____

_____

Ex. 2.24

David Morris, Plumbing Supplier

Error 1

(a) _____

_____

(b)   **General Journal**

Date	Particulars	Fol	Debit $	Credit $

(c) _____

_____

_____

Error 2

(a) _____

_____

_____

(b)   **General Journal**

Date	Particulars	Fol	Debit $	Credit $

(c) _____

_____

_____

Ex. 2.24

Error 3

(a) _____

_____

_____

(b)   General Journal

Date	Particulars	Fol	Debit $	Credit $

(c) _____

_____

_____

Error 4

(a) _____

_____

_____

(b)   General Journal

Date	Particulars	Fol	Debit $	Credit $

(c) _____

_____

Ex. 2.24

Error 5

(a)

(b)   General Journal

Date	Particulars	Fol	Debit $	Credit $

(c)

Error 6

(a)

(b)   General Journal

Date	Particulars	Fol	Debit $	Credit $

(c)

Ex. 2.25

B Graham
General Journal

Date	Particulars	Fol	Debit $	Credit $

Ex. 2.26 (a)

J Watson, Retailer
General Journal

Date	Particulars	Fol	Debit $	Credit $

Ex. 2.26 (a)

J Watson, Retailer
General Journal

Date	Particulars	Fol	Debit $	Credit $

Ex. 2.26 (b)

J Watson, Retailer
General Ledger (only accounts affected by balance day adjustments)
Accounts Receivable Control Account

Date	Particulars	Fol	Debit $	Credit $	Balance $

GST Collected Account

Date	Particulars	Fol	Debit $	Credit $	Balance $

Ex. 2.26 (b)

J Watson, Retailer
General Ledger (only accounts affected by balance day adjustments)
Stock of Office Consumables Account

Date	Particulars	Fol	Debit $	Credit $	Balance $

Sales Account

Date	Particulars	Fol	Debit $	Credit $	Balance $

Purchases of Office Consumables Account

Date	Particulars	Fol	Debit $	Credit $	Balance $

Accumulated Depreciation – Motor Vehicles Account

Date	Particulars	Fol	Debit $	Credit $	Balance $

Insurance Account

Date	Particulars	Fol	Debit $	Credit $	Balance $

Bad Debts Account

Date	Particulars	Fol	Debit $	Credit $	Balance $

Ex. 2.26 (b)

J Watson, Retailer
General Ledger (only accounts affected by balance day adjustments)
Interest Income Account

Date	Particulars	Fol	Debit $	Credit $	Balance $

Allowance for Doubtful Debts Account

Date	Particulars	Fol	Debit $	Credit $	Balance $

Salaries Account

Date	Particulars	Fol	Debit $	Credit $	Balance $

Prepaid Expenses Account

Date	Particulars	Fol	Debit $	Credit $	Balance $

Cost of Office Consumables Used Account

Date	Particulars	Fol	Debit $	Credit $	Balance $

Depreciation – Motor Vehicles Account

Date	Particulars	Fol	Debit $	Credit $	Balance $

Depreciation – Furniture Account

Date	Particulars	Fol	Debit $	Credit $	Balance $

Accumulated Depreciation – Furniture Account

Date	Particulars	Fol	Debit $	Credit $	Balance $

Ex. 2.26 (b)

J Watson, Retailer
General Ledger (only accounts affected by balance day adjustments)
Annual Leave Expense Account

Date	Particulars	Fol	Debit $	Credit $	Balance $

Provision for Annual Leave Expense Account

Date	Particulars	Fol	Debit $	Credit $	Balance $

Long-Service Leave Expense Account

Date	Particulars	Fol	Debit $	Credit $	Balance $

Provision for Long-Service Leave Account

Date	Particulars	Fol	Debit $	Credit $	Balance $

Accrued Income Account

Date	Particulars	Fol	Debit $	Credit $	Balance $

Doubtful Debts Expense Account

Date	Particulars	Fol	Debit $	Credit $	Balance $

Accrued Expenses Account

Date	Particulars	Fol	Debit $	Credit $	Balance $

Ex. 2.26 (c)	Debit $	Credit $
J Watson, Retailer		
Final Trial Balance as at 30 June 2017		
Account name		

Ex. 2.27 (a)	Solution in textbook.				
	N Schmidt				
	General Journal				
Date	Particulars		Fol	Debit $	Credit $

Ex. 2.27 (b)	Solution in textbook.				
	N Schmidt				
	General Ledger (only accounts affected by balance day adjustments)				
	Advertising Account				
Date	Particulars	Fol	Debit $	Credit $	Balance $
	Commission Income Account				
Date	Particulars	Fol	Debit $	Credit $	Balance $
	Accounts Payable Control Account				
Date	Particulars	Fol	Debit $	Credit $	Balance $
	Interest on Loan Account				
Date	Particulars	Fol	Debit $	Credit $	Balance $
	Accumulated Depreciation – Furniture Account				
Date	Particulars	Fol	Debit $	Credit $	Balance $
	Purchases Account				
Date	Particulars	Fol	Debit $	Credit $	Balance $
	Rent Account				
Date	Particulars	Fol	Debit $	Credit $	Balance $

Ex. 2.27 (b)	Solution in textbook.				

N Schmidt
General Ledger (only accounts affected by balance day adjustments)
Provision for Annual Leave Account

Date	Particulars	Fol	Debit $	Credit $	Balance $

Provision for Long Service Leave Account

Date	Particulars	Fol	Debit $	Credit $	Balance $

GST Collected Account

Date	Particulars	Fol	Debit $	Credit $	Balance $

GST Paid Account

Date	Particulars	Fol	Debit $	Credit $	Balance $

Depreciation – Motor Vehicles Account

Date	Particulars	Fol	Debit $	Credit $	Balance $

Accumulated Depreciation – Motor Vehicles Account

Date	Particulars	Fol	Debit $	Credit $	Balance $

Depreciation – Furniture Account

Date	Particulars	Fol	Debit $	Credit $	Balance $

Ex. 2.27 (b)   Solution in textbook.

N Schmidt
General Ledger (only accounts affected by balance day adjustments)
Accrued Expenses Account

Date	Particulars	Fol	Debit $	Credit $	Balance $

Prepaid Expenses Account

Date	Particulars	Fol	Debit $	Credit $	Balance $

Annual Leave Expense Account

Date	Particulars	Fol	Debit $	Credit $	Balance $

Long Service Leave Expense Account

Date	Particulars	Fol	Debit $	Credit $	Balance $

Accrued Income Account

Date	Particulars	Fol	Debit $	Credit $	Balance $

Ex. 2.27 (c) Solution in textbook.		
N Schmidt		
Final Trial Balance as at 30 June 2018		
Account name	**Debit** **$**	**Credit** **$**

Ex. 2.28				
	W Lake			
	General Journal			
Date	Particulars	Fol	Debit $	Credit $

Ex. 2.28

W Lake
General Journal

Date	Particulars	Fol	Debit $	Credit $

Ex. 2.29				Debit $	Credit $
	C Hillier, Retailer				
	General Journal				
Date	Particulars		Fol		

Ex. 2.29

C Hillier, Retailer
General Journal

Date	Particulars	Fol	Debit $	Credit $

Ex. 3.1	Explain reasons for closing the ledger at the end of each accounting period.			
Ex. 3.2 (a)	Briefly explain profit determination accounts.			
Ex. 3.2 (b)	Briefly explain closing entries.			
Ex. 3.2 (c)	Briefly explain cost of sales.			
Ex. 3.2 (d)	Briefly explain opening stock.			
Ex. 3.2 (e)	Briefly explain closing stock.			
Ex. 3.3	Why do retailers/wholesalers prepare a Trading account?			
Ex. 3.4 (a)	Briefly explain gross profit or loss.			
Ex. 3.4 (b)	Briefly explain net profit or loss.			
Ex. 3.5	What is a post-closing trial balance?			

Ex. 3.6 (a)	Solution in textbook.			
	Hayes Retailers			
	General Journal			
Date	Particulars	Fol	Debit $	Credit $

Ex. 3.6 (b)					
Hayes Retailers					
General Ledger					
Cash at Bank Account					
Date	Particulars	Fol	Debit $	Credit $	Balance $

Capital – C Hayes Account					
Date	Particulars	Fol	Debit $	Credit $	Balance $

Drawings – C Hayes Account					
Date	Particulars	Fol	Debit $	Credit $	Balance $

Accounts Receivable Control Account					
Date	Particulars	Fol	Debit $	Credit $	Balance $

Accounts Payable Control Account					
Date	Particulars	Fol	Debit $	Credit $	Balance $

Stock Account					
Date	Particulars	Fol	Debit $	Credit $	Balance $

Furniture and Fittings – at Cost Account					
Date	Particulars	Fol	Debit $	Credit $	Balance $

| Ex. 3.6 (b) | Solution in textbook. | | | | |

Hayes Retailers
General Ledger
Accumulated Depreciation – Furniture and Fittings Account

Date	Particulars	Fol	Debit $	Credit $	Balance $

Land and Buildings – at Cost Account

Date	Particulars	Fol	Debit $	Credit $	Balance $

Purchases Account

Date	Particulars	Fol	Debit $	Credit $	Balance $

Purchases Returns and Allowances Account

Date	Particulars	Fol	Debit $	Credit $	Balance $

Customs Duty on Purchases Account

Date	Particulars	Fol	Debit $	Credit $	Balance $

Sales Account

Date	Particulars	Fol	Debit $	Credit $	Balance $

Insurance Account

Date	Particulars	Fol	Debit $	Credit $	Balance $

Ex. 3.6 (b)	Solution in textbook.				

Hayes Retailers
General Ledger
Discount Allowed Account

Date	Particulars	Fol	Debit $	Credit $	Balance $

Depreciation – Furniture and Fittings Account

Date	Particulars	Fol	Debit $	Credit $	Balance $

Discount Income Account

Date	Particulars	Fol	Debit $	Credit $	Balance $

Interest on Overdraft Account

Date	Particulars	Fol	Debit $	Credit $	Balance $

Cartage Inwards Account

Date	Particulars	Fol	Debit $	Credit $	Balance $

Bad Debts Account

Date	Particulars	Fol	Debit $	Credit $	Balance $

Sales Returns and Allowances Account

Date	Particulars	Fol	Debit $	Credit $	Balance $

Ex. 3.6 (b)	Solution in textbook.				

Hayes Retailers
General Ledger
Advertising Account

Date	Particulars	Fol	Debit $	Credit $	Balance $

Salaries Account

Date	Particulars	Fol	Debit $	Credit $	Balance $

EFTPOS and Credit Card Merchant Fees Account

Date	Particulars	Fol	Debit $	Credit $	Balance $

Cartage Outwards Account

Date	Particulars	Fol	Debit $	Credit $	Balance $

Electricity Account

Date	Particulars	Fol	Debit $	Credit $	Balance $

Rent Expense Account

Date	Particulars	Fol	Debit $	Credit $	Balance $

Plant and Equipment – at Cost Account

Date	Particulars	Fol	Debit $	Credit $	Balance $

Ex. 3.6 (b)	Solution in textbook.				
	Hayes Retailers				
	General Ledger				
	Accumulated Depreciation – Plant and Equipment Account				
Date	Particulars	Fol	Debit $	Credit $	Balance $
	Depreciation – Plant and Equipment Account				
Date	Particulars	Fol	Debit $	Credit $	Balance $
	Accrued Expenses Account				
Date	Particulars	Fol	Debit $	Credit $	Balance $
	Loan – Jones Account				
Date	Particulars	Fol	Debit $	Credit $	Balance $
	Interest on Loan – Jones Account				
Date	Particulars	Fol	Debit $	Credit $	Balance $
	GST Collected Account				
Date	Particulars	Fol	Debit $	Credit $	Balance $
	GST Paid Account				
Date	Particulars	Fol	Debit $	Credit $	Balance $
	Depreciation – Buildings Account				
Date	Particulars	Fol	Debit $	Credit $	Balance $
	Accumulated Depreciation – Buildings Account				
Date	Particulars	Fol	Debit $	Credit $	Balance $

Ex. 3.6 (b)   Solution in textbook.

Hayes Retailers
General Ledger
Trading Account

Date	Particulars	Fol	Debit $	Credit $	Balance $

Profit and Loss Account

Date	Particulars	Fol	Debit $	Credit $	Balance $

Ex. 3.7 (a)				
	Scotts Suppliers			
	General Journal			
Date	Particulars	Fol	Debit $	Credit $

Ex. 3.7 (b)					
Scotts Suppliers					
General Ledger					
Drawings – C Scott Account					
Date	Particulars	Fol	Debit $	Credit $	Balance $

Stock Account					
Date	Particulars	Fol	Debit $	Credit $	Balance $

Accounts Payable Control Account					
Date	Particulars	Fol	Debit $	Credit $	Balance $

Purchases Account					
Date	Particulars	Fol	Debit $	Credit $	Balance $

Purchases Returns Account					
Date	Particulars	Fol	Debit $	Credit $	Balance $

Sales Account					
Date	Particulars	Fol	Debit $	Credit $	Balance $

Rent Expense Account					
Date	Particulars	Fol	Debit $	Credit $	Balance $

Insurance Account					
Date	Particulars	Fol	Debit $	Credit $	Balance $

Ex. 3.7 (b)					
Scotts Suppliers					
General Ledger					
Cartage Inward Account					
Date	Particulars	Fol	**Debit** $	**Credit** $	**Balance** $
Capital – C Scott Account					
Date	Particulars	Fol	**Debit** $	**Credit** $	**Balance** $
Cash at Bank Account					
Date	Particulars	Fol	**Debit** $	**Credit** $	**Balance** $
Sales Returns Account					
Date	Particulars	Fol	**Debit** $	**Credit** $	**Balance** $
Discount Expense Account					
Date	Particulars	Fol	**Debit** $	**Credit** $	**Balance** $
Discount Income Account					
Date	Particulars	Fol	**Debit** $	**Credit** $	**Balance** $
Equipment – at Cost Account					
Date	Particulars	Fol	**Debit** $	**Credit** $	**Balance** $
Freight Outwards Account					
Date	Particulars	Fol	**Debit** $	**Credit** $	**Balance** $

Ex. 3.7 (b)					
Scotts Suppliers					
General Ledger					
Depreciation – Equipment Account					
Date	Particulars	Fol	Debit $	Credit $	Balance $
Accumulated Depreciation – Equipment Account					
Date	Particulars	Fol	Debit $	Credit $	Balance $
Petty Cash Advance Account					
Date	Particulars	Fol	Debit $	Credit $	Balance $
Loan – S King Account					
Date	Particulars	Fol	Debit $	Credit $	Balance $
Interest on Loan – S King Account					
Date	Particulars	Fol	Debit $	Credit $	Balance $
GST Collected Account					
Date	Particulars	Fol	Debit $	Credit $	Balance $
GST Paid Account					
Date	Particulars	Fol	Debit $	Credit $	Balance $
Accrued Income Account					
Date	Particulars	Fol	Debit $	Credit $	Balance $
Prepaid Expenses Account					
Date	Particulars	Fol	Debit $	Credit $	Balance $

Ex. 3.7 (b)					
Scotts Suppliers					
General Ledger					
Lease Payments – Vehicles Account					
Date	Particulars	Fol	**Debit** $	**Credit** $	**Balance** $
Trading Account					
Date	Particulars	Fol	**Debit** $	**Credit** $	**Balance** $
Profit and Loss Account					
Date	Particulars	Fol	**Debit** $	**Credit** $	**Balance** $

Ex. 3.8 (a)				
	Harry's Hardware			
	General Journal			
Date	Particulars	Fol	Debit $	Credit $

Ex. 3.8 (b)

Harry's Hardware
General Ledger

Cash at Bank Account

Date	Particulars	Fol	Debit $	Credit $	Balance $

Investments Account

Date	Particulars	Fol	Debit $	Credit $	Balance $

Allowance for Doubtful Debts Account

Date	Particulars	Fol	Debit $	Credit $	Balance $

Stock Account

Date	Particulars	Fol	Debit $	Credit $	Balance $

Motor Vehicles – at Cost Account

Date	Particulars	Fol	Debit $	Credit $	Balance $

Accumulated Depreciation – Motor Vehicles Account

Date	Particulars	Fol	Debit $	Credit $	Balance $

Depreciation – Furniture and Fittings Account

Date	Particulars	Fol	Debit $	Credit $	Balance $

Sales Account

Date	Particulars	Fol	Debit $	Credit $	Balance $

Ex. 3.8 (b)

Harry's Hardware
General Ledger
Sales Returns Account

Date	Particulars	Fol	Debit $	Credit $	Balance $

Rent Expense Account

Date	Particulars	Fol	Debit $	Credit $	Balance $

Goodwill Account

Date	Particulars	Fol	Debit $	Credit $	Balance $

Rent Income Account

Date	Particulars	Fol	Debit $	Credit $	Balance $

Cartage Outwards Account

Date	Particulars	Fol	Debit $	Credit $	Balance $

Discount Expense Account

Date	Particulars	Fol	Debit $	Credit $	Balance $

Cost of Stationery Used Account

Date	Particulars	Fol	Debit $	Credit $	Balance $

Ex. 3.8 (b)

Harry's Hardware

General Ledger

Drawings – H Taylor Account

Date	Particulars	Fol	Debit $	Credit $	Balance $

Depreciation – Motor Vehicles Account

Date	Particulars	Fol	Debit $	Credit $	Balance $

Furniture and Fittings – at Cost Account

Date	Particulars	Fol	Debit $	Credit $	Balance $

Discount Income Account

Date	Particulars	Fol	Debit $	Credit $	Balance $

Purchases Account

Date	Particulars	Fol	Debit $	Credit $	Balance $

Purchases Returns Account

Date	Particulars	Fol	Debit $	Credit $	Balance $

Cartage Inwards Account

Date	Particulars	Fol	Debit $	Credit $	Balance $

Ex. 3.8 (b)					

Harry's Hardware
General Ledger
Accumulated Depreciation – Furniture and Fittings Account

Date	Particulars	Fol	Debit $	Credit $	Balance $

Accounts Receivable Control Account

Date	Particulars	Fol	Debit $	Credit $	Balance $

Accounts Payable Control Account

Date	Particulars	Fol	Debit $	Credit $	Balance $

GST Collected Account

Date	Particulars	Fol	Debit $	Credit $	Balance $

GST Paid Account

Date	Particulars	Fol	Debit $	Credit $	Balance $

Stock of Stationery on Hand Account

Date	Particulars	Fol	Debit $	Credit $	Balance $

Advertising Account

Date	Particulars	Fol	Debit $	Credit $	Balance $

Bad Debts Account

Date	Particulars	Fol	Debit $	Credit $	Balance $

Ex. 3.8 (b)					

Harry's Hardware
General Ledger
Doubtful Debts Account

Date	Particulars	Fol	Debit $	Credit $	Balance $

Prepaid Expenses Account

Date	Particulars	Fol	Debit $	Credit $	Balance $

Accrued Expenses Account

Date	Particulars	Fol	Debit $	Credit $	Balance $

Prepaid Income Account

Date	Particulars	Fol	Debit $	Credit $	Balance $
30-Jun-18					

Capital – H Taylor Account

Date	Particulars	Fol	Debit $	Credit $	Balance $

Trading Account

Date	Particulars	Fol	Debit $	Credit $	Balance $

Ex. 3.8 (b)

Harry's Hardware
General Ledger
Profit and Loss Account

Date	Particulars	Fol	Debit $	Credit $	Balance $

Ex. 3.8 (c)		
Harry's Hardware		
Post-closing trial balance as at 30 June 2018		
Account name	Debit $	Credit $

Ex. 3.8 (d)

Harry's Hardware

Statement of Financial Position as at 30 June 2018

Assets	$		$	$	$	$
Owner's Equity						
	$ Liabilities					

Exercise 3.8 (d)

Ex. 3.9 (a) & (c)				
	Surprise Importers			
	General Journal			
Date	Particulars	Fol	Debit $	Credit $

Ex. 3.9 (a) & (c)				
Surprise Importers				
General Journal				
Date	Particulars	Fol	Debit $	Credit $

Ex. 3.9 (a) & (c)

Surprise Importers
General Journal

Date	Particulars	Fol	Debit $	Credit $

Ex. 3.9 (b) & (d)

Surprise Importers
General Ledger
Rent Expense Account

Date	Particulars	Fol	Debit $	Credit $	Balance $

Loss on Sale of Furniture Account

Date	Particulars	Fol	Debit $	Credit $	Balance $

Accounts Receivable Control Account

Date	Particulars	Fol	Debit $	Credit $	Balance $

Advertising Account

Date	Particulars	Fol	Debit $	Credit $	Balance $

Discount Expense Account

Date	Particulars	Fol	Debit $	Credit $	Balance $

Motor Vehicles – at Cost Account

Date	Particulars	Fol	Debit $	Credit $	Balance $

Furniture and Fittings – at Cost Account

Date	Particulars	Fol	Debit $	Credit $	Balance $

Ex. 3.9 (b) & (d)					

Surprise Importers

General Ledger

Accumulated Depreciation – Furniture and Fittings Account

Date	Particulars	Fol	Debit $	Credit $	Balance $

Allowance for Doubtful Debts Account

Date	Particulars	Fol	Debit $	Credit $	Balance $

Stock of Stationery on Hand Account

Date	Particulars	Fol	Debit $	Credit $	Balance $

Purchases of Stationery Account

Date	Particulars	Fol	Debit $	Credit $	Balance $

Wages Account

Date	Particulars	Fol	Debit $	Credit $	Balance $

Insurance Account

Date	Particulars	Fol	Debit $	Credit $	Balance $

Discount Income Account

Date	Particulars	Fol	Debit $	Credit $	Balance $

Ex. 3.9 (b) & (d)

Surprise Importers
General Ledger
Cash at Bank Account

Date	Particulars	Fol	Debit $	Credit $	Balance $

Accounts Payable Control Account

Date	Particulars	Fol	Debit $	Credit $	Balance $

Capital – J Bartel Account

Date	Particulars	Fol	Debit $	Credit $	Balance $

Sales Account

Date	Particulars	Fol	Debit $	Credit $	Balance $

Purchases Account

Date	Particulars	Fol	Debit $	Credit $	Balance $

Stock Account

Date	Particulars	Fol	Debit $	Credit $	Balance $

Accrued Wages Expenses Account

Date	Particulars	Fol	Debit $	Credit $	Balance $

Ex. 3.9 (b) & (d)					

Surprise Importers
General Ledger
Cartage Inwards Account

Date	Particulars	Fol	Debit $	Credit $	Balance $

Duty and Wharfage Account

Date	Particulars	Fol	Debit $	Credit $	Balance $

Drawings – J Bartel Account

Date	Particulars	Fol	Debit $	Credit $	Balance $

GST Collected Account

Date	Particulars	Fol	Debit $	Credit $	Balance $

GST Paid Account

Date	Particulars	Fol	Debit $	Credit $	Balance $

Prepaid Expenses Account

Date	Particulars	Fol	Debit $	Credit $	Balance $

Accrued Advertising Expenses Account

Date	Particulars	Fol	Debit $	Credit $	Balance $

Ex. 3.9 (b) & (d)

Surprise Importers

General Ledger

Depreciation – Furniture and Fittings Account

Date	Particulars	Fol	Debit $	Credit $	Balance $

Depreciation – Motor Vehicles Account

Date	Particulars	Fol	Debit $	Credit $	Balance $

Accumulated Depreciation – Motor Vehicles Account

Date	Particulars	Fol	Debit $	Credit $	Balance $

Doubtful Debts Account

Date	Particulars	Fol	Debit $	Credit $	Balance $

Accrued Income Account

Date	Particulars	Fol	Debit $	Credit $	Balance $

Commission Income Account

Date	Particulars	Fol	Debit $	Credit $	Balance $

Cost of Stationery Used Account

Date	Particulars	Fol	Debit $	Credit $	Balance $

Ex. 3.9 (b) & (d)

Surprise Importers
General Ledger
Trading Account

Date	Particulars	Fol	Debit $	Credit $	Balance $

Profit and Loss Account

Date	Particulars	Fol	Debit $	Credit $	Balance $

Ex. 3.9 (e)		
Surprise Importers		
Post-closing trial balance as at 30 June 2017		
Account name	**Debit** **$**	**Credit** **$**

Ex. 3.9 (f)

Surprise Importers
Statement of Financial Position as at 30 June 2017

Assets	$	$	Liabilities	$	$	$
			Owner's equity			

Exercise 3.9 (f)

Ex. 3.10 (a) & (c)				
B Castle, Gardener				
General Journal				
Date	Particulars	Fol	Debit $	Credit $

Ex. 3.10 (a) & (c)

B Castle, Gardener
General Journal

Date	Particulars	Fol	Debit $	Credit $

Ex. 3.10 (b) & (d)

B Castle, Gardener
General Ledger
Cash at Bank Account

Date	Particulars	Fol	Debit $	Credit $	Balance $

Fees Income Account

Date	Particulars	Fol	Debit $	Credit $	Balance $

Motor Mowers – at Cost Account

Date	Particulars	Fol	Debit $	Credit $	Balance $

Accumulated Depreciation – Motor Mowers Account

Date	Particulars	Fol	Debit $	Credit $	Balance $

Trailer – at Cost Account

Date	Particulars	Fol	Debit $	Credit $	Balance $

Accumulated Depreciation – Trailer Account

Date	Particulars	Fol	Debit $	Credit $	Balance $

Accounts Receivable Control Account

Date	Particulars	Fol	Debit $	Credit $	Balance $

Ex. 3.10 (b) & (d)

B Castle, Gardener
General Ledger
Loss on Sale of Mower Account

Date	Particulars	Fol	Debit $	Credit $	Balance $

Wages Account

Date	Particulars	Fol	Debit $	Credit $	Balance $

Petrol and Oil Account

Date	Particulars	Fol	Debit $	Credit $	Balance $

Repairs and Maintenance Account

Date	Particulars	Fol	Debit $	Credit $	Balance $

Insurance Account

Date	Particulars	Fol	Debit $	Credit $	Balance $

Lease Payments – Motor Vehicle Account

Date	Particulars	Fol	Debit $	Credit $	Balance $

Gardening Equipment – at Cost Account

Date	Particulars	Fol	Debit $	Credit $	Balance $

Ex. 3.10 (b) & (d)

B Castle, Gardener
General Ledger
Accumulated Depreciation – Gardening Equipment Account

Date	Particulars	Fol	Debit $	Credit $	Balance $

Capital – B Castle Account

Date	Particulars	Fol	Debit $	Credit $	Balance $

Drawings – B Castle Account

Date	Particulars	Fol	Debit $	Credit $	Balance $

GST Collected Account

Date	Particulars	Fol	Debit $	Credit $	Balance $

GST Paid Account

Date	Particulars	Fol	Debit $	Credit $	Balance $

Vehicle Expenses Account

Date	Particulars	Fol	Debit $	Credit $	Balance $

Allowance for Doubtful Debts Account

Date	Particulars	Fol	Debit $	Credit $	Balance $

Ex. 3.10 (b) & (d)

B Castle, Gardener
General Ledger
Advertising Account

Date	Particulars	Fol	Debit $	Credit $	Balance $

Interest Income Account

Date	Particulars	Fol	Debit $	Credit $	Balance $

Accrued Expenses Account

Date	Particulars	Fol	Debit $	Credit $	Balance $

Depreciation – Motor Mowers Account

Date	Particulars	Fol	Debit $	Credit $	Balance $

Depreciation – Trailer Account

Date	Particulars	Fol	Debit $	Credit $	Balance $

Depreciation – Gardening Equipment Account

Date	Particulars	Fol	Debit $	Credit $	Balance $

Bad Debts Account

Date	Particulars	Fol	Debit $	Credit $	Balance $

Ex. 3.10 (b) & (d)

B Castle, Gardener
General Ledger
Doubtful Debts Account

Date	Particulars	Fol	Debit $	Credit $	Balance $

Profit and Loss Account

Date	Particulars	Fol	Debit $	Credit $	Balance $

Ex. 3.10 (e)

B Castle, Gardener
Post-closing trial balance as at 30 June 2017

Account name	Debit $	Credit $

Date	Particulars	Fol	Debit $	Credit $
Ex. 3.11 (a) & (c) Solution in textbook.				
B Wow, Poodle Groomer				
General Journal				

Ex. 3.11 (a) & (c) Solution in textbook.

B Wow, Poodle Groomer
General Journal

Date	Particulars	Fol	Debit $	Credit $

Ex. 3.11 (b) & (d) Solution in textbook.					
B Wow, Poodle Groomer					
General Ledger					
Drawings – B Wow Account					
Date	Particulars	Fol	Debit $	Credit $	Balance $
Accounts Receivable Control Account					
Date	Particulars	Fol	Debit $	Credit $	Balance $
Accounts Payable Control Account					
Date	Particulars	Fol	Debit $	Credit $	Balance $
Cash at Bank Account					
Date	Particulars	Fol	Debit $	Credit $	Balance $
Stock of Grooming Supplies Account					
Date	Particulars	Fol	Debit $	Credit $	Balance $
Purchases of Grooming Supplies Account					
Date	Particulars	Fol	Debit $	Credit $	Balance $
Grooming Fees Income Account					
Date	Particulars	Fol	Debit $	Credit $	Balance $

Ex. 3.11 (b) & (d)   Solution in textbook.

B Wow, Poodle Groomer
General Ledger
Grooming Equipment – at Cost Account

Date	Particulars	Fol	Debit $	Credit $	Balance $

Accumulated Depreciation – Grooming Equipment Account

Date	Particulars	Fol	Debit $	Credit $	Balance $

Commission Income on Sale of Dog Accessories Account

Date	Particulars	Fol	Debit $	Credit $	Balance $

Wages Account

Date	Particulars	Fol	Debit $	Credit $	Balance $

Power and Light Account

Date	Particulars	Fol	Debit $	Credit $	Balance $

Rent Expense Account

Date	Particulars	Fol	Debit $	Credit $	Balance $

Motor Vehicles – at Cost Account

Date	Particulars	Fol	Debit $	Credit $	Balance $

Ex. 3.11 (b) & (d)   Solution in textbook.

B Wow, Poodle Groomer
General Ledger
Accumulated Depreciation – Motor Vehicles Account

Date	Particulars	Fol	Debit $	Credit $	Balance $

Motor Vehicle Expenses Account

Date	Particulars	Fol	Debit $	Credit $	Balance $

Insurance Account

Date	Particulars	Fol	Debit $	Credit $	Balance $

Legal Fees Account

Date	Particulars	Fol	Debit $	Credit $	Balance $

GST Collected Account

Date	Particulars	Fol	Debit $	Credit $	Balance $

GST Paid Account

Date	Particulars	Fol	Debit $	Credit $	Balance $

Capital – B Wow Account

Date	Particulars	Fol	Debit $	Credit $	Balance $

Ex. 3.11 (b) & (d)   Solution in textbook.

B Wow, Poodle Groomer
General Ledger
Accrued Expenses Account

Date	Particulars	Fol	Debit $	Credit $	Balance $

Depreciation – Motor Vehicles Account

Date	Particulars	Fol	Debit $	Credit $	Balance $

Depreciation – Grooming Equipment Account

Date	Particulars	Fol	Debit $	Credit $	Balance $

Prepaid Expenses Account

Date	Particulars	Fol	Debit $	Credit $	Balance $

Accrued Income Account

Date	Particulars	Fol	Debit $	Credit $	Balance $

Cost of Grooming Supplies Used Account

Date	Particulars	Fol	Debit $	Credit $	Balance $

Ex. 3.11 (b) & (d)   Solution in textbook.

B Wow, Poodle Groomer
General Ledger
Profit and Loss Account

Date	Particulars	Fol	Debit $	Credit $	Balance $

Ex. 3.11 (e) Solution in textbook.

B Wow, Poodle Groomer
Post-closing trial balance as at 30 June 2017

Ex. 3.12   Briefly explain reversal entries.

_____

_____

_____

Ex. 3.13   Outline where reversal entries fit into the recording sequence at balance date.

_____

_____

_____

Ex. 3.14   Which balance day adjustments are reversed?   Why?

_____

_____

_____

Ex. 3.15   Which balance day adjustments are not reversed? Why?

_____

_____

_____

Ex. 3.16 (a) & (b)

A Large, Retailer
General Journal

Date	Particulars	Fol	Debit $	Credit $

Ex. 3.16 (a) & (b)

A Large, Retailer
General Journal

Date	Particulars	Fol	Debit $	Credit $

Ex. 3.17 (a) & (b)

Spot Off Cleaning Service
General Journal

Date	Particulars	Fol	Debit $	Credit $

Ex. 3.17 (a) & (b)

Spot Off Cleaning Service
General Journal

Date	Particulars	Fol	Debit $	Credit $

Ex. 3.18 (a), (b) & (d) Solution in textbook.

Smithy's Timber and Hardware Supplies
General Journal

Date	Particulars	Fol	Debit $	Credit $

Ex. 3.18 (a), (b) & (d) Solution in textbook.

Smithy's Timber and Hardware Supplies
General Journal

Date	Particulars	Fol	Debit $	Credit $

Ex. 3.18 (a), (b) & (d) Solution in textbook.

Smithy's Timber and Hardware Supplies
General Journal

Date	Particulars	Fol	Debit $	Credit $

Ex. 3.18 (a), (b) & (d) Solution in textbook.

Smithy's Timber and Hardware Supplies
General Journal

Date	Particulars	Fol	Debit $	Credit $

Ex. 3.18 (a), (b) & (d) Solution in textbook.

Smithy's Timber and Hardware Supplies
General Ledger
Cash at Bank Account

Date	Particulars	Fol	Debit $	Credit $	Balance $

Capital – G Smith Account

Date	Particulars	Fol	Debit $	Credit $	Balance $

Sales Account

Date	Particulars	Fol	Debit $	Credit $	Balance $

GST Collected Account

Date	Particulars	Fol	Debit $	Credit $	Balance $

GST Paid Account

Date	Particulars	Fol	Debit $	Credit $	Balance $

Purchases Account

Date	Particulars	Fol	Debit $	Credit $	Balance $

Ex. 3.18 (a), (b) & (d) Solution in textbook.

Smithy's Timber and Hardware Supplies
General Ledger
Investments – Aussie Bonds Account

Date	Particulars	Fol	Debit $	Credit $	Balance $

Drawings – G Smith Account

Date	Particulars	Fol	Debit $	Credit $	Balance $

Discount Income Account

Date	Particulars	Fol	Debit $	Credit $	Balance $

Discount Expense Account

Date	Particulars	Fol	Debit $	Credit $	Balance $

Accounts Receivable Control Account

Date	Particulars	Fol	Debit $	Credit $	Balance $

Accounts Payable Control Account

Date	Particulars	Fol	Debit $	Credit $	Balance $

Cartage Inwards Account

Date	Particulars	Fol	Debit $	Credit $	Balance $

Ex. 3.18 (a), (b) & (d) Solution in textbook.					
Smithy's Timber and Hardware Supplies					
General Ledger					
Purchases Returns Account					
Date	Particulars	Fol	Debit $	Credit $	Balance $
Cartage Outwards Account					
Date	Particulars	Fol	Debit $	Credit $	Balance $
Sales Returns Account					
Date	Particulars	Fol	Debit $	Credit $	Balance $
Interest Income on Aussie Bonds Account					
Date	Particulars	Fol	Debit $	Credit $	Balance $
Land and Buildings – at Cost Account					
Date	Particulars	Fol	Debit $	Credit $	Balance $
Mortgage Loan on Land and Buildings Account					
Date	Particulars	Fol	Debit $	Credit $	Balance $
Advertising Account					
Date	Particulars	Fol	Debit $	Credit $	Balance $

Ex. 3.18 (a), (b) & (d) Solution in textbook.					
Smithy's Timber and Hardware Supplies					
General Ledger					
Vehicle Expenses Account					
			Debit $	Credit $	Balance $
Date	Particulars	Fol			

Rates Account					
			Debit $	Credit $	Balance $
Date	Particulars	Fol			

Insurance Account					
			Debit $	Credit $	Balance $
Date	Particulars	Fol			

Bad Debts Account					
			Debit $	Credit $	Balance $
Date	Particulars	Fol			

Vehicles – at Cost Account					
			Debit $	Credit $	Balance $
Date	Particulars	Fol			

Accumulated Depreciation – Vehicles Account					
			Debit $	Credit $	Balance $
Date	Particulars	Fol			

Ex. 3.18 (a), (b) & (d) Solution in textbook.					
Smithy's Timber and Hardware Supplies					
General Ledger					
Salaries Account					
Date	Particulars	Fol	Debit $	Credit $	Balance $
EFTPOS and Credit Card Merchant Fees Account					
Date	Particulars	Fol	Debit $	Credit $	Balance $
Office Expenses Account					
Date	Particulars	Fol	Debit $	Credit $	Balance $
Equipment – at Cost Account					
Date	Particulars	Fol	Debit $	Credit $	Balance $
Accumulated Depreciation – Equipment Account					
Date	Particulars	Fol	Debit $	Credit $	Balance $
Allowance for Doubtful Debts Account					
Date	Particulars	Fol	Debit $	Credit $	Balance $

Ex. 3.18 (a), (b) & (d) Solution in textbook.					
Smithy's Timber and Hardware Supplies					
General Ledger					
Stock Account					
Date	Particulars	Fol	Debit $	Credit $	Balance $
Interest Expense on Mortgage Loan Account					
Date	Particulars	Fol	Debit $	Credit $	Balance $
Accumulated Depreciation – Buildings Account					
Date	Particulars	Fol	Debit $	Credit $	Balance $
Prepaid Expenses Account					
Date	Particulars	Fol	Debit $	Credit $	Balance $
Accrued Expenses Account					
Date	Particulars	Fol	Debit $	Credit $	Balance $
Depreciation – Buildings Account					
Date	Particulars	Fol	Debit $	Credit $	Balance $
Depreciation – Vehicles Account					
Date	Particulars	Fol	Debit $	Credit $	Balance $

Ex. 3.18 (a), (b) & (d) Solution in textbook.					
Smithy's Timber and Hardware Supplies					
General Ledger					
Depreciation – Equipment Account					
Date	Particulars	Fol	Debit $	Credit $	Balance $
Long Service Leave Account					
Date	Particulars	Fol	Debit $	Credit $	Balance $
Provision for Long Service Leave Account					
Date	Particulars	Fol	Debit $	Credit $	Balance $
Accrued Income Account					
Date	Particulars	Fol	Debit $	Credit $	Balance $
Doubtful Debts Account					
Date	Particulars	Fol	Debit $	Credit $	Balance $
Annual Leave Account					
Date	Particulars	Fol	Debit $	Credit $	Balance $
Provision for Annual Leave Account					
Date	Particulars	Fol	Debit $	Credit $	Balance $

Ex. 3.18 (a), (b) & (d) Solution in textbook.

Smithy's Timber and Hardware Supplies
General Ledger
Trading Account

Date	Particulars	Fol	Debit $	Credit $	Balance $

Profit and Loss Account

Date	Particulars	Fol	Debit $	Credit $	Balance $

Ex. 3.18 (c) Solution in textbook.		
Smithy's Timber and Hardware Supplies		
Post-closing trial balance as at 30 June 2016		
Account name	Debit $	Credit $

Ex. 3.19 (a), (b) & (d)

F Bait, Wholesaler
General Journal

Date	Particulars	Fol	Debit $	Credit $

Ex. 3.19 (a), (b) & (d)

F Bait, Wholesaler
General Journal

Date	Particulars	Fol	Debit $	Credit $

Ex. 3.19 (a), (b) & (d)

F Bait, Wholesaler
General Journal

Date	Particulars	Fol	Debit $	Credit $

Ex. 3.19 (a), (b) & (d)

F Bait, Wholesaler
General Journal

Date	Particulars	Fol	Debit $	Credit $

Ex. 3.19 (a), (b) & (d)

F Bait, Wholesaler
General Ledger
Capital – F Bait Account

Date	Particulars	Fol	Debit $	Credit $	Balance $

Sales Account

Date	Particulars	Fol	Debit $	Credit $	Balance $

Cash at Bank Account

Date	Particulars	Fol	Debit $	Credit $	Balance $

Purchases Account

Date	Particulars	Fol	Debit $	Credit $	Balance $

Stock Account

Date	Particulars	Fol	Debit $	Credit $	Balance $

Sales Returns Account

Date	Particulars	Fol	Debit $	Credit $	Balance $

Purchases Returns Account

Date	Particulars	Fol	Debit $	Credit $	Balance $

Ex. 3.19 (a), (b) & (d)					
F Bait, Wholesaler					
General Ledger					
GST Collected Account					
Date	Particulars	Fol	**Debit $**	**Credit $**	**Balance $**
GST Paid Account					
Date	Particulars	Fol	**Debit $**	**Credit $**	**Balance $**
Drawings – A Mina Account					
Date	Particulars	Fol	**Debit $**	**Credit $**	**Balance $**
Accounts Receivable Control Account					
Date	Particulars	Fol	**Debit $**	**Credit $**	**Balance $**
Accounts PayableControl Account					
Date	Particulars	Fol	**Debit $**	**Credit $**	**Balance $**
Cartage Inwards Account					
Date	Particulars	Fol	**Debit $**	**Credit $**	**Balance $**
Rates and Taxes Account					
Date	Particulars	Fol	**Debit $**	**Credit $**	**Balance $**
Loan – Loose Finance Account					
Date	Particulars	Fol	**Debit $**	**Credit $**	**Balance $**

Ex. 3.19 (a), (b) & (d)					

F Bait, Wholesaler

General Ledger

Land & Buildings – at Cost Account

Date	Particulars	Fol	Debit $	Credit $	Balance $

Discount Expense Account

Date	Particulars	Fol	Debit $	Credit $	Balance $

Bad Debts Account

Date	Particulars	Fol	Debit $	Credit $	Balance $

Profit on Sale of Vehicle Account

Date	Particulars	Fol	Debit $	Credit $	Balance $

Accumulated Depreciation – Vehicles Account

Date	Particulars	Fol	Debit $	Credit $	Balance $

Vehicles – at Cost Account

Date	Particulars	Fol	Debit $	Credit $	Balance $

Buying Expenses Account

Date	Particulars	Fol	Debit $	Credit $	Balance $

Ex. 3.19 (a), (b) & (d)

F Bait, Wholesaler
General Ledger
Provision for Annual Leave Account

Date	Particulars	Fol	Debit $	Credit $	Balance $

Wages Account

Date	Particulars	Fol	Debit $	Credit $	Balance $

Petty Cash Advance Account

Date	Particulars	Fol	Debit $	Credit $	Balance $

Interest on Loan Account

Date	Particulars	Fol	Debit $	Credit $	Balance $

Advertising Account

Date	Particulars	Fol	Debit $	Credit $	Balance $

Insurance on Stock Account

Date	Particulars	Fol	Debit $	Credit $	Balance $

Ex. 3.19 (a), (b) & (d)					
F Bait, Wholesaler					
General Ledger					
Commission Income Account					
Date	Particulars	Fol	Debit $	Credit $	Balance $
Selling Expenses Account					
Date	Particulars	Fol	Debit $	Credit $	Balance $
Allowance for Doubtful Debts Account					
Date	Particulars	Fol	Debit $	Credit $	Balance $
Purchases of Packaging Materials Account					
Date	Particulars	Fol	Debit $	Credit $	Balance $
Stock of Packaging Materials Account					
Date	Particulars	Fol	Debit $	Credit $	Balance $
Prepaid Expenses Account					
Date	Particulars	Fol	Debit $	Credit $	Balance $

Ex. 3.19 (a), (b) & (d)

F Bait Wholesaler
General Ledger
Accrued Expenses Account

Date	Particulars	Fol	Debit $	Credit $	Balance $

Cost of Packaging Materials Used Account

Date	Particulars	Fol	Debit $	Credit $	Balance $

Depreciation – Vehicles Account

Date	Particulars	Fol	Debit $	Credit $	Balance $

Long Service Leave Expense Account

Date	Particulars	Fol	Debit $	Credit $	Balance $

Provision for Long Service Leave Account

Date	Particulars	Fol	Debit $	Credit $	Balance $

Annual Leave Expense Account

Date	Particulars	Fol	Debit $	Credit $	Balance $

Personal Leave Expense Account

Date	Particulars	Fol	Debit $	Credit $	Balance $

Ex. 3.19 (a), (b) & (d)

F Bait, Wholesaler
General Ledger
Provision for Personal Leave Account

Date	Particulars	Fol	Debit $	Credit $	Balance $

Doubtful Debts Account

Date	Particulars	Fol	Debit $	Credit $	Balance $

Prepaid Income Account

Date	Particulars	Fol	Debit $	Credit $	Balance $

Depreciation – Buildings Account

Date	Particulars	Fol	Debit $	Credit $	Balance $

Accumulated Depreciation – Buildings Account

Date	Particulars	Fol	Debit $	Credit $	Balance $

Trading Account

Date	Particulars	Fol	Debit $	Credit $	Balance $

Ex. 3.19 (a), (b) & (d)					
F Bait, Wholesaler					
General Ledger					
Profit and Loss Account					
Date	Particulars	Fol	Debit $	Credit $	Balance $

Ex. 3.19 (c)		
F Bait, Wholesaler		
Post-closing trial balance as at 30 June 2019		
Account name	**Debit $**	**Credit $**

Ex. 3.20 (a) & (b)				
Fisher's Anglers' Supplies				
General Journal				
Date	Particulars	Fol	Debit $	Credit $

Ex. 3.20 (a) & (b)				
	Fisher's Anglers' Supplies			
	General Journal			
Date	Particulars	Fol	Debit $	Credit $

Ex. 3.20 (a) & (b)

Fisher's Anglers' Supplies
General Ledger
Cash at Bank Account

Date	Particulars	Fol	Debit $	Credit $	Balance $

Petty Cash Advance Account

Date	Particulars	Fol	Debit $	Credit $	Balance $

Accrued Wages – Salespersons Account

Date	Particulars	Fol	Debit $	Credit $	Balance $

EFTPOS and Credit Card Merchant Fees Account

Date	Particulars	Fol	Debit $	Credit $	Balance $

Accounts Receivable Control Account

Date	Particulars	Fol	Debit $	Credit $	Balance $

Accounts Payable Control Account

Date	Particulars	Fol	Debit $	Credit $	Balance $

Cartage Inward Account

Date	Particulars	Fol	Debit $	Credit $	Balance $

Cartage Outward Account

Date	Particulars	Fol	Debit $	Credit $	Balance $

Ex. 3.20 (a) & (b)

Fisher's Anglers' Supplies
General Ledger
Depreciation – Buildings Account

Date	Particulars	Fol	Debit $	Credit $	Balance $

Accumulated Depreciation – Buildings Account

Date	Particulars	Fol	Debit $	Credit $	Balance $

Capital – J Fisher Account

Date	Particulars	Fol	Debit $	Credit $	Balance $

Drawings – J Fisher Account

Date	Particulars	Fol	Debit $	Credit $	Balance $

Interest Income Account

Date	Particulars	Fol	Debit $	Credit $	Balance $

Land and Buildings – at Cost Account

Date	Particulars	Fol	Debit $	Credit $	Balance $

Bad Debts Account

Date	Particulars	Fol	Debit $	Credit $	Balance $

Ex. 3.20 (a) & (b)

Fisher's Anglers' Supplies
General Ledger
Loan from J Harbour Account

Date	Particulars	Fol	Debit $	Credit $	Balance $

Depreciation – Delivery Vehicles Account

Date	Particulars	Fol	Debit $	Credit $	Balance $

Commission – Salespersons Account

Date	Particulars	Fol	Debit $	Credit $	Balance $

Wages – Salespersons Account

Date	Particulars	Fol	Debit $	Credit $	Balance $

Sales Returns Account

Date	Particulars	Fol	Debit $	Credit $	Balance $

Purchases Returns Account

Date	Particulars	Fol	Debit $	Credit $	Balance $

Depreciation – Office Equipment Account

Date	Particulars	Fol	Debit $	Credit $	Balance $

Ex. 3.20 (a) & (b)

Fisher's Anglers' Supplies
General Ledger
Discount Expense Account

Date	Particulars	Fol	Debit $	Credit $	Balance $

Discount Income Account

Date	Particulars	Fol	Debit $	Credit $	Balance $

Sales Account

Date	Particulars	Fol	Debit $	Credit $	Balance $

Purchases Account

Date	Particulars	Fol	Debit $	Credit $	Balance $

Accumulated Depreciation – Office Equipment Account

Date	Particulars	Fol	Debit $	Credit $	Balance $

Office Equipment – at Cost Account

Date	Particulars	Fol	Debit $	Credit $	Balance $

Advertising Account

Date	Particulars	Fol	Debit $	Credit $	Balance $

Ex. 3.20 (a) & (b)

Fisher's Anglers' Supplies
Accrued Interest Income Account

Date	Particulars	Fol	Debit $	Credit $	Balance $

Interest on Loan Account

Date	Particulars	Fol	Debit $	Credit $	Balance $

Accumulated Depreciation – Delivery Vehicles Account

Date	Particulars	Fol	Debit $	Credit $	Balance $

Delivery Vehicles – at Cost Account

Date	Particulars	Fol	Debit $	Credit $	Balance $

Office Wages Account

Date	Particulars	Fol	Debit $	Credit $	Balance $

Stock Account

Date	Particulars	Fol	Debit $	Credit $	Balance $

Delivery Expenses Account

Date	Particulars	Fol	Debit $	Credit $	Balance $

Ex. 3.20 (a) & (b)

Fisher's Anglers' Supplies
General Ledger
Prepaid Advertising Account

Date	Particulars	Fol	Debit $	Credit $	Balance $

Insurance – General Account

Date	Particulars	Fol	Debit $	Credit $	Balance $

Insurance – Delivery Vehicles Account

Date	Particulars	Fol	Debit $	Credit $	Balance $

Trading Account

Date	Particulars	Fol	Debit $	Credit $	Balance $

Ex. 3.20 (a) & (b)

Fisher's Anglers' Supplies
General Ledger
Profit and Loss Account

Date	Particulars	Fol	Debit $	Credit $	Balance $

Ex. 3.21 (a) (b) & (d)

F Costalota, Fruit Wholesaler
General Journal

Date	Particulars	Fol	Debit $	Credit $

Ex. 3.21 (a) (b) & (d)

F Costalota, Fruit Wholesaler
General Journal

Date	Particulars	Fol	Debit $	Credit $

Ex. 3.21 (a) (b) & (d)

F Costalota, Fruit Wholesaler
General Journal

Date	Particulars	Fol	Debit $	Credit $

Ex. 3.21 (a) (b) & (d)

F Costalota, Fruit Wholesaler
General Ledger
Loan from Readymade Finance Account

Date	Particulars	Fol	Debit $	Credit $	Balance $

Purchases of Fruit Account

Date	Particulars	Fol	Debit $	Credit $	Balance $

Sales of Fruit Account

Date	Particulars	Fol	Debit $	Credit $	Balance $

Drawings – F Costalota Account

Date	Particulars	Fol	Debit $	Credit $	Balance $

Goodwill Account

Date	Particulars	Fol	Debit $	Credit $	Balance $

Wages Account

Date	Particulars	Fol	Debit $	Credit $	Balance $

Shop Fixtures and Fittings – at Cost Account

Date	Particulars	Fol	Debit $	Credit $	Balance $

Accumulated Depreciation – Shop Fixtures and Fittings Account

Date	Particulars	Fol	Debit $	Credit $	Balance $

Ex. 3.21 (a) (b) & (d)

F Costalota, Fruit Wholesaler
General Ledger
Stock Account

Date	Particulars	Fol	Debit $	Credit $	Balance $

Bank Account

Date	Particulars	Fol	Debit $	Credit $	Balance $

Electricity Account

Date	Particulars	Fol	Debit $	Credit $	Balance $

Refrigeration Equipment – at Cost Account

Date	Particulars	Fol	Debit $	Credit $	Balance $

Accumulated Depreciation – Refrigeration Equipment Account

Date	Particulars	Fol	Debit $	Credit $	Balance $

Motor Vehicle – at Cost Account

Date	Particulars	Fol	Debit $	Credit $	Balance $

Accumulated Depreciation – Motor Vehicle Account

Date	Particulars	Fol	Debit $	Credit $	Balance $

Ex. 3.21 (a) (b) & (d)

F Costalota, Fruit Wholesaler
General Ledger
Accounts Payable Control Account

Date	Particulars	Fol	Debit $	Credit $	Balance $

Accounts Receivable Control Account

Date	Particulars	Fol	Debit $	Credit $	Balance $

Allowance for Doubtful Debts Account

Date	Particulars	Fol	Debit $	Credit $	Balance $

Motor Vehicle Expenses Account

Date	Particulars	Fol	Debit $	Credit $	Balance $

Office Expenses Account

Date	Particulars	Fol	Debit $	Credit $	Balance $

Advertising Account

Date	Particulars	Fol	Debit $	Credit $	Balance $

GST Collected Account

Date	Particulars	Fol	Debit $	Credit $	Balance $

Ex. 3.21 (a) (b) & (d)

F Costalota, Fruit Wholesaler
General Ledger
GST Paid Account

Date	Particulars	Fol	Debit $	Credit $	Balance $

Insurance Account

Date	Particulars	Fol	Debit $	Credit $	Balance $

Capital – F Costalota Account

Date	Particulars	Fol	Debit $	Credit $	Balance $

Interest Expense Account

Date	Particulars	Fol	Debit $	Credit $	Balance $

Accrued Expenses Account

Date	Particulars	Fol	Debit $	Credit $	Balance $

Prepaid Expenses Account

Date	Particulars	Fol	Debit $	Credit $	Balance $

Ex. 3.21 (a) (b) & (d)

F Costalota, Fruit Wholesaler
General Ledger
Depreciation – Refrigeration Equipment Account

Date	Particulars	Fol	Debit $	Credit $	Balance $

Depreciation – Shop Fixtures and Fittings Account

Date	Particulars	Fol	Debit $	Credit $	Balance $

Depreciation – Motor Vehicles Account

Date	Particulars	Fol	Debit $	Credit $	Balance $

Bad Debts Account

Date	Particulars	Fol	Debit $	Credit $	Balance $

Doubtful Debts Account

Date	Particulars	Fol	Debit $	Credit $	Balance $

Annual Leave Expense Account

Date	Particulars	Fol	Debit $	Credit $	Balance $

Provision for Annual Leave Account

Date	Particulars	Fol	Debit $	Credit $	Balance $

Ex. 3.21 (a) (b) & (d)

F Costalota, Fruit Wholesaler
General Ledger
Trading Account

Date	Particulars	Fol	Debit $	Credit $	Balance $

Profit and Loss Account

Date	Particulars	Fol	Debit $	Credit $	Balance $

Ex. 3.21 (c)

F Costalota, Fruit Wholesaler
Post-closing trial balance as at 30 June 2016

Account name	Debit $	Credit $

Ex. 3.22 (a) (b) & (d) Solution in textbook.				
Spring Clean Dry Cleaners				
General Journal				
Date	Particulars	Fol	Debit $	Credit $

Ex. 3.22 (a) (b) & (d) Solution in textbook.				
Spring Clean Dry Cleaners				
General Journal				
Date	Particulars	Fol	Debit $	Credit $

Ex. 3.22 (a) (b) & (d) Solution in textbook.

Spring Clean Dry Cleaners
General Journal

Date	Particulars	Fol	Debit $	Credit $

Ex. 3.22 (a) (b) & (d) Solution in textbook.					
Spring Clean Dry Cleaners					
General Ledger					
Shop Furniture and Equipment – at Cost Account					
Date	Particulars	Fol	Debit $	Credit $	Balance $
Accumulated Depreciation – Shop Furniture and Equipment Account					
Date	Particulars	Fol	Debit $	Credit $	Balance $
Capital – A Shiny Account					
Date	Particulars	Fol	Debit $	Credit $	Balance $
Dry Cleaning Equipment – at Cost Account					
Date	Particulars	Fol	Debit $	Credit $	Balance $
Dry Cleaning Equipment Running Expenses Account					
Date	Particulars	Fol	Debit $	Credit $	Balance $
Maintenance of Dry Cleaning Equipment Account					
Date	Particulars	Fol	Debit $	Credit $	Balance $
Dry Cleaning Income Account					
Date	Particulars	Fol	Debit $	Credit $	Balance $

Ex. 3.22 (a) (b) & (d) Solution in textbook.

Spring Clean Dry Cleaners
General Ledger
Stock of Dry Cleaning Fluids Account

Date	Particulars	Fol	Debit $	Credit $	Balance $

Purchases of Dry Cleaning Fluids Account

Date	Particulars	Fol	Debit $	Credit $	Balance $

Wages – Dry Cleaning Staff Account

Date	Particulars	Fol	Debit $	Credit $	Balance $

Wages – Shop Staff Account

Date	Particulars	Fol	Debit $	Credit $	Balance $

EFTPOS and Credit Card Merchant Fees Account

Date	Particulars	Fol	Debit $	Credit $	Balance $

Rent of Premises Account

Date	Particulars	Fol	Debit $	Credit $	Balance $

Salaries – Office Staff Account

Date	Particulars	Fol	Debit $	Credit $	Balance $

Ex. 3.22 (a) (b) & (d) Solution in textbook.

Spring Clean Dry Cleaners
General Ledger
Office Expenses Account

Date	Particulars	Fol	Debit $	Credit $	Balance $

Accounts Payable Control Account

Date	Particulars	Fol	Debit $	Credit $	Balance $

Drawings – A Shiny Account

Date	Particulars	Fol	Debit $	Credit $	Balance $

Office Equipment – at Cost Account

Date	Particulars	Fol	Debit $	Credit $	Balance $

Cash at Bank Account

Date	Particulars	Fol	Debit $	Credit $	Balance $

Petty Cash Advance Account

Date	Particulars	Fol	Debit $	Credit $	Balance $

Accumulated Depreciation – Dry Cleaning Equipment Account

Date	Particulars	Fol	Debit $	Credit $	Balance $

Ex. 3.22 (a) (b) & (d) Solution in textbook.

Spring Clean Dry Cleaners
General Ledger
Provision for Long Service Leave Account

Date	Particulars	Fol	Debit $	Credit $	Balance $

Legal Expenses Account

Date	Particulars	Fol	Debit $	Credit $	Balance $

Shares in Precision Instruments Ltd Account

Date	Particulars	Fol	Debit $	Credit $	Balance $

Accounts Receivable Control Account

Date	Particulars	Fol	Debit $	Credit $	Balance $

Accumulated Depreciation – Office Equipment Account

Date	Particulars	Fol	Debit $	Credit $	Balance $

Discount Income Account

Date	Particulars	Fol	Debit $	Credit $	Balance $

Advertising Account

Date	Particulars	Fol	Debit $	Credit $	Balance $

Ex. 3.22 (a) (b) & (d) Solution in textbook.

Spring Clean Dry Cleaners
General Ledger
Wrapping Materials and Coat Hangers Expense Account

Date	Particulars	Fol	Debit $	Credit $	Balance $

Allowance for Doubtful Debts Account

Date	Particulars	Fol	Debit $	Credit $	Balance $

GST Collected Account

Date	Particulars	Fol	Debit $	Credit $	Balance $

GST Paid Account

Date	Particulars	Fol	Debit $	Credit $	Balance $

Cost of Dry Cleaning Fluids Used Account

Date	Particulars	Fol	Debit $	Credit $	Balance $

Depreciation – Dry Cleaning Equipment Account

Date	Particulars	Fol	Debit $	Credit $	Balance $

Ex. 3.22 (a) (b) & (d) Solution in textbook.

Spring Clean Dry Cleaners
General Ledger
Depreciation – Office Equipment Account

Date	Particulars	Fol	Debit $	Credit $	Balance $

Depreciation – Shop Furniture and Equipment Account

Date	Particulars	Fol	Debit $	Credit $	Balance $

Prepaid Expenses Account

Date	Particulars	Fol	Debit $	Credit $	Balance $

Accrued Income Account

Date	Particulars	Fol	Debit $	Credit $	Balance $

Dividends Income Account

Date	Particulars	Fol	Debit $	Credit $	Balance $

Long Service Leave Expense Account

Date	Particulars	Fol	Debit $	Credit $	Balance $

Doubtful Debts Account

Date	Particulars	Fol	Debit $	Credit $	Balance $

Ex. 3.22 (a) (b) & (d) Solution in textbook.

Spring Clean Dry Cleaners
General Ledger
Accrued Expenses Account

Date	Particulars	Fol	Debit $	Credit $	Balance $

Profit and Loss Account

Date	Particulars	Fol	Debit $	Credit $	Balance $

Ex. 3.22 (c) Solution in textbook.

Spring Clean Dry Cleaners
Post-closing trial balance as at 30 June 2018

Account name	Debit $	Credit $

Ex. 3.23 (a), (b) & (d)				
	C Meredith, Builder			
	General Journal			
Date	Particulars	Fol	Debit $	Credit $

Ex. 3.23 (a), (b) & (d)

C Meredith, Builder
General Journal

Date	Particulars	Fol	Debit $	Credit $

Ex. 3.23 (a), (b) & (d)

C Meredith, Builder
General Journal

Date	Particulars	Fol	Debit $	Credit $

Ex. 3.23 (a), (b) & (d)

C Meredith, Builder
General Ledger
Provision for Long Service Leave Account

Date	Particulars	Fol	Debit $	Credit $	Balance $

Equipment – at Cost Account

Date	Particulars	Fol	Debit $	Credit $	Balance $

Accumulated Depreciation – Equipment Account

Date	Particulars	Fol	Debit $	Credit $	Balance $

Motor Vehicle – at Cost Account

Date	Particulars	Fol	Debit $	Credit $	Balance $

Accumulated Depreciation – Motor Vehicle Account

Date	Particulars	Fol	Debit $	Credit $	Balance $

Interest on Loan – B Stewart Account

Date	Particulars	Fol	Debit $	Credit $	Balance $

Repairs and Maintenance – Motor Vehicle Account

Date	Particulars	Fol	Debit $	Credit $	Balance $

Ex. 3.23 (a), (b) & (d)

C Meredith, Builder
General Ledger
Capital – C Meredith Account

Date	Particulars	Fol	Debit $	Credit $	Balance $

Registration and Insurance Account

Date	Particulars	Fol	Debit $	Credit $	Balance $

Cash at Bank Account

Date	Particulars	Fol	Debit $	Credit $	Balance $

Building Fees Account

Date	Particulars	Fol	Debit $	Credit $	Balance $

Sundry Office Expenses Account

Date	Particulars	Fol	Debit $	Credit $	Balance $

Drawings – C Meredith Account

Date	Particulars	Fol	Debit $	Credit $	Balance $

Ex. 3.23 (a), (b) & (d)

C Meredith, Builder
General Ledger
Accounts Receivable Control Account

Date	Particulars	Fol	Debit $	Credit $	Balance $

Stock of Materials and Supplies Account

Date	Particulars	Fol	Debit $	Credit $	Balance $

Wages Account

Date	Particulars	Fol	Debit $	Credit $	Balance $

Building Permits and Charges Account

Date	Particulars	Fol	Debit $	Credit $	Balance $

Loan – B Stewart Account

Date	Particulars	Fol	Debit $	Credit $	Balance $

Purchases of Materials and Supplies Account

Date	Particulars	Fol	Debit $	Credit $	Balance $

Ex. 3.23 (a), (b) & (d)

C Meredith, Builder
General Ledger
Advertising Account

Date	Particulars	Fol	Debit $	Credit $	Balance $

Creditors Account

Date	Particulars	Fol	Debit $	Credit $	Balance $

GST Collected Account

Date	Particulars	Fol	Debit $	Credit $	Balance $

GST Paid Account

Date	Particulars	Fol	Debit $	Credit $	Balance $

Allowance for Doubtful Debts Account

Date	Particulars	Fol	Debit $	Credit $	Balance $

Prepaid Expenses Account

Date	Particulars	Fol	Debit $	Credit $	Balance $

Ex. 3.23 (a), (b) & (d)

C Meredith, Builder
General Ledger
Cost of Materials and Supplies Used Account

Date	Particulars	Fol	Debit $	Credit $	Balance $

Long Service Leave Expense Account

Date	Particulars	Fol	Debit $	Credit $	Balance $

Depreciation – Equipment Account

Date	Particulars	Fol	Debit $	Credit $	Balance $

Accrued Expenses Account

Date	Particulars	Fol	Debit $	Credit $	Balance $

Depreciation – Motor Vehicle Account

Date	Particulars	Fol	Debit $	Credit $	Balance $

Doubtful Debts Account

Date	Particulars	Fol	Debit $	Credit $	Balance $

Ex. 3.23 (a), (b) & (d)					
C Meredith, Builder					
General Ledger					
Bad Debts Account					
Date	**Particulars**	**Fol**	**Debit $**	**Credit $**	**Balance $**
Profit and Loss Account					
Date	**Particulars**	**Fol**	**Debit $**	**Credit $**	**Balance $**

Ex. 3.23 (c)

C Meredith, Builder
Post-closing trial balance as at 31 December 2017

Account name	Debit $	Credit $

Ex. 4.1 (a)			
Pete's Pizza			
Statement of comprehensive income for the month ended 31 October 2016			
	$	$	$

Ex. 4.1 (a)

Pete's Pizza
Statement of comprehensive income for the month ended 31 October 2016 (continued)

	$	$	$

Ex. 4.1 (b)				
Pete's Pizza				
Statement of financial position as at 31 October 2016				
		$	$	$

Ex. 4.2 (a)				
Fisher's Anglers' Supplies				
Statement of comprehensive income for the year ended 30 June 2017				
	$	$	$	$

Ex. 4.2 (a)

Fisher's Anglers' Supplies
Statement of comprehensive income for the year ended 30 June 2017 (continued)

	$	$	$	$

Ex. 4.2 (b)				
Fisher's Anglers' Supplies				
Statement of financial position as at 30 June 2017				
	$	$	$	$

Ex. 4.3 (a) Solution in textbook.				
Jolly Plumbing Supplies				
Statement of comprehensive income for year ended 30 June 2018				
	$	$	$	$

Ex. 4.3 (a) Solution in textbook.

Jolly Plumbing Supplies
Statement of comprehensive income for year ended 30 June 2018 (continued)

	$	$	$	$

Notes accompanying statement of comprehensive income

_____

_____

_____

_____

_____

_____

Ex. 4.3 (b) Solution in textbook.				
Jolly Plumbing Supplies				
Statement of financial position as at 30 June 2018				
	$	$	$	$

Ex. 4.4 (a)

Bob's Game Centre
Statement of comprehensive income for the year ended 30 June 2017

	$	$	$

Ex. 4.4 (a)

Bob's Game Centre
Statement of comprehensive income for the year ended 30 June 2017 (continued)

	$	$	$

Notes accompanying statement of comprehensive income

_____

_____

_____

_____

_____

_____

Ex. 4.4 (b)

Bob's Game Centre
Statement of financial position as at 30 June 2017

	$	$	$	$

Ex. 4.5 (a)

R Garfoot, Gardener
Statement of comprehensive income for year ended 30 June 2017

	$	$	$

Ex. 4.5 (a)

R Garfoot, Gardener
Statement of comprehensive income for year ended 30 June 2017 (continued)

	$	$	$

Notes accompanying statement of comprehensive income

_____

_____

_____

_____

_____

_____

_____

Ex. 4.5 (b)

R Garfoot, Gardener
Statement of financial position as at 30 June 2017

	$	$	$	$

Ex. 4.6 (a)

Brent's Office Supplies

Financial statements worksheet for year ended 30 June 2017

| Account name | Trial balance before adjustments | | Balance day adjustments | | Adjusted trial balance | | Statement of comprehensive income | | | | Statement of financial position | |
| | | | | | | | Trading | | Profit and loss | | | |
	Debit	Credit	Debit	Credit	Debit	Credit	Debit	Credit	Debit	Credit	Debit	Credit

Ex. 4.6 (a)

Brent's Office Supplies
Financial statements worksheet for year ended 30 June 2017

| Account name | Trial balance before adjustments | | Balance day adjustments | | Adjusted trial balance | | Statement of comprehensive income | | | | Statement of financial position | |
| | | | | | | | Trading | | Profit and loss | | | |
	Debit	Credit	Debit	Credit	Debit	Credit	Debit	Credit	Debit	Credit	Debit	Credit

Balance day adjustments:

Exercise 4.6 (a) (2)

Ex. 4.6 (b)

Brent's Office Supplies
Statement of comprehensive income for the year ended 30 June 2017

	$	$	$	$

Ex. 4.6 (b)

Brent's Office Supplies

Statement of comprehensive income for the year ended 30 June 2017 (continued)

	$	$	$	$

Notes accompanying statement of comprehensive income

_____

_____

_____

_____

Ex. 4.6 (c)

Brent's Office Supplies
Statement of financial position as at 30 June 2017

	$	$	$	$

Ex. 4.7 (a)

Alsonetti Wholesalers

Financial statements worksheet for 6 months ended 30 June 2018

Account name	Trial balance before adjustments		Balance day adjustments		Adjusted trial balance		Statement of comprehensive income				Statement of financial position	
							Trading		Profit and loss			
	Debit	Credit	Debit	Credit	Debit	Credit	Debit	Credit	Debit	Credit	Debit	Credit

Exercise 4.7 (a)

Ex. 4.7 (a)

Alsonetti Wholesalers

Financial statements worksheet for 6 months ended 30 June 2018 (continued)

| Account name | Trial balance before adjustments | | Balance day adjustments | | Adjusted trial balance | | Statement of comprehensive income | | | | Statement of financial position | |
| | | | | | | | Trading | | Profit and loss | | | |
	Debit	Credit	Debit	Credit	Debit	Credit	Debit	Credit	Debit	Credit	Debit	Credit

Balance day adjustments:

Exercise 4.7 (a) (2)

Ex. 4.7 (b)					
Alsonetti Wholesalers					
Statement of comprehensive income for 6 months ended 30 June 2018					
		$	$	$	$

Ex. 4.7 (b)

Alsonetti Wholesalers
Statement of comprehensive income for 6 months ended 30 June 2018 (continued)

	$	$	$	$

Ex. 4.7 (c)				
Alsonetti Wholesalers				
Statement of financial position at at 30 June 2018				
	$	$	$	$

Ex. 4.8 (a)

Watling's Timber and Hardware Supplies
Financial statements worksheet for year ended 30 June 2018

Account name	Trial balance before adjustments		Balance day adjustments		Adjusted trial balance		Statement of comprehensive income				Statement of financial position	
							Trading		Profit and loss			
	Debit	Credit	Debit	Credit	Debit	Credit	Debit	Credit	Debit	Credit	Debit	Credit

Exercise 4.8 (a)

Ex. 4.8 (a)

Watling's Timber and Hardware Supplies
Financial statements worksheet for year ended 30 June 2018

Account name	Trial balance before adjustments		Balance day adjustments		Adjusted trial balance		Statement of comprehensive income				Statement of financial position	
							Trading		Profit and loss			
	Debit	Credit	Debit	Credit	Debit	Credit	Debit	Credit	Debit	Credit	Debit	Credit

Balance day adjustments

Ex. 4.8 (b)

Watling's Timber and Hardware Supplies
Statement of comprehensive income for the year ended 30 June 2018

	$	$	$	$

Ex. 4.8 (b)

Watling's Timber and Hardware Supplies
Statement of comprehensive income for the year ended 30 June 2018 (continued)

	$	$	$	$

Notes accompanying statement of comprehensive income

_____

_____

_____

_____

Ex. 4.8 (c)

Watling's Timber and Hardware Supplies
Statement of financial position as at 30 June 2018

	$	$	$	$

Ex. 4.9 (a)

Solution in textbook.

Claudius Imports
Financial statements worksheet for year ended 31 December 2018

Account name	Trial balance before adjustments		Balance day adjustments		Adjusted trial balance		Statement of comprehensive income				Statement of financial position	
							Trading		Profit and loss			
	Debit	Credit	Debit	Credit	Debit	Credit	Debit	Credit	Debit	Credit	Debit	Credit

Ex. 4.9 (a)

Solution in textbook.

Claudius Imports

Financial statements worksheet for year ended 31 December 2018

| Account name | Trial balance before adjustments | | Balance day adjustments | | Adjusted trial balance | | Statement of comprehensive income | | | | Statement of financial position | |
| | | | | | | | Trading | | Profit and loss | | | |
	Debit	Credit	Debit	Credit	Debit	Credit	Debit	Credit	Debit	Credit	Debit	Credit

Balance day adjustments

Exercise 4.9 (a) (2)

Ex. 4.9 (b) Solution in textbook.

Claudius Imports
Statement of comprehensive income for the year ended 31 December 2018

	$	$	$	$

Ex. 4.9 (b) Solution in textbook.

Claudius Imports

Statement of comprehensive income for the year ended 31 December 2018 (continued)

	$	$	$	$

Notes accompanying statement of comprehensive income

Ex. 4.9 (c) Solution in textbook.

Claudius Imports
Statement of financial position as at 31 December 2018

	$	$	$	$

Ex. 4.10 (a)

Lovely Rita's Health Clinic
Financial statements worksheet for year ended ended 30 June 2017

Account name	Trial balance before adjustments		Balance day adjustments		Adjusted trial balance		Statement of comprehensive income		Statement of financial position	
	Debit	Credit	Debit	Credit	Debit	Credit	Debit	Credit	Debit	Credit

Exercise 4.10 (a)

Ex. 4.10 (a)

Lovely Rita's Health Clinic

Financial statements worksheet for year ended ended 30 June 2017

Account name	Trial balance before adjustments		Balance day adjustments		Adjusted trial balance		Statement of comprehensive income		Statement of financial position	
	Debit	Credit	Debit	Credit	Debit	Credit	Debit	Credit	Debit	Credit

Balance day adjustments:

_____

_____

_____

_____

Exercise 4.10 (a) (2)

Ex. 4.10 (b)

Lovely Rita's Health Clinic
Statement of comprehensive income for the year ended 30 June 2017

	$	$	$

Ex. 4.10 (b)

Lovely Rita's Health Clinic
Statement of comprehensive income for the year ended 30 June 2017 (continued)

	$	$	$

Notes accompanying statement of comprehensive income

_____

_____

_____

_____

_____

_____

_____

_____

Ex. 4.10 (c)

Lovely Rita's Health Clinic
Statement of financial position as at 30 June 2017

	$	$	$	$

Ex. 4.11 (a) Solution in textbook.

Spring Clean Dry Cleaners
Financial statements worksheet for the year ended 30 June 2018

Account name	Trial balance before adjustments		Balance day adjustments		Adjusted trial balance		Statement of comprehensive Income		Statement of financial position	
	Debit	Credit	Debit	Credit	Debit	Credit	Debit	Credit	Debit	Credit

Exercise 4.11 (a)

Ex. 4.11 (a) Solution in textbook.

Spring Clean Dry Cleaners
Financial statements worksheet for the year ended 30 June 2018

Account name	Trial balance before adjustments		Balance day adjustments		Adjusted trial balance		Statement of comprehensive income		Statement of financial position	
	Debit	Credit	Debit	Credit	Debit	Credit	Debit	Credit	Debit	Credit

Balance day adjustments

Exercise 4.11 (a) (2)

Ex. 4.11 (b) Solution in textbook.

Spring Clean Dry Cleaners
Statement of comprehensive income for the year ended 30 June 2018

	$	$	$

Ex. 4.11 (b) Solution in textbook.

Spring Clean Dry Cleaners
Statement of comprehensive income for the year ended 30 June 2018 (continued)

	$	$	$

Notes accompanying statement of comprehensive income

Ex. 4.11 (c) Solution in textbook.

Spring Clean Dry Cleaners
Statement of financial position as at 30 June 2018

	$	$	$	$

Ex. 4.12 (a)

J Van Dort, Builder

Financial statements worksheet for the year ended December 2017

Account name	Trial balance before adjustments		Balance day adjustments		Adjusted trial balance		Statement of comprehensive income		Statement of financial position	
	Debit	Credit	Debit	Credit	Debit	Credit	Debit	Credit	Debit	Credit

Exercise 4.12 (a)

Ex. 4.12 (a)

J Van Dort, Builder

Financial statements worksheet for the year ended December 2017

Account Name	Trial balance before adjustments		Balance day adjustments		Adjusted trial balance		Statement of comprehensive income		Statement of financial position	
	Debit	Credit	Debit	Credit	Debit	Credit	Debit	Credit	Debit	Credit

Balance day adjustments

_____

_____

_____

_____

_____

Exercise 4.12 (a) (2)

Ex. 4.12 (b)

C Meredith, Builder
Statement of comprehensive income for the year ended 31 December 2017

	$	$	$

Notes accompanying statement of comprehensive income

_____

_____

_____

_____

Ex. 4.12 (c)

C Meredith, Builder
Statement of financial position as at 31 December 2017

	$	$	$	$

Ex. 5.1 Briefly distinguish between the following terms.

Current assets

_____

_____

Non-current assets

_____

_____

_____

Ex. 5.2 What are property, plant and equipment? Explain.

_____

_____

Ex. 5.3 Briefly outline control procedures over property, plant and equipment.

_____

_____

_____

_____

_____

_____

Ex. 5.4 Solution in textbook.

(a) _____   (e) _____

(b) _____   (f) _____

(c) _____   (g) _____

(d) _____   (h) _____

Ex. 5.5

(a) _____

(b) _____

(c) _____

(d) _____

(e) _____

(f) _____

Ex. 5.6

Depreciation is essentially the recognition and allocation of the expired service potential of an asset.' Comment on the validity of this statement.

_____

_____

_____

_____

Ex. 5.7   Solution in textbook.
(a)   Depreciation – Fixtures and Fittings

_____

Depreciation – Delivery Vehicle

_____

(b)   **C Vulture, Chemist**
                                 General Journal

Date	Particulars	Fol	Debit $	Credit $

(c)   **C Mixture, Chemist**
                                 General Ledger
            Accumulated Depreciation – Fixtures and Fittings Account

Date	Particulars	Debit $	Credit $	Balance $

Accumulated Depreciation – Delivery Vehicle Account

Date	Particulars	Debit $	Credit $	Balance $

Depreciation – Fixtures and Fittings Account

Date	Particulars	Debit $	Credit $	Balance $

Depreciation – Delivery Vehicle Account

Date	Particulars	Debit $	Credit $	Balance $

Ex. 5.8   Depreciation on computer for year ended 30 June 2018.

Ex. 5.9

Gertie's Garden Creations
Purchases Journal

Date	Creditor	Ref	Purchases $	Sundries Amount $	Sundries Account	GST paid $	Accounts payable control $

Sales Journal

Date	Debtor	Ref	Sales	Sundries Amount	Sundries Account	GST collected	Accounts receivable control

General Journal

Date	Particulars	Debit $	Credit $

Ex. 5.10   Solution in textbook.

Koochew Enterprises

(a)   **Sales Journal**

Date	Debtor	Ref	Sales $	Sundries Amount $	Sundries Account	GST collected $	Accounts receivable control $

General Journal

Date	Particulars	Debit $	Credit $

(b)   **General Ledger (extract)**
                        Sale of Non-Current Assets Account

Date	Particulars	Fol	Debit $	Credit $	Balance $

Ex. 5.11 (a)   Stewart Distributors
                                                            Purchases Journal

Date	Creditor	Ref	Purchases $	Sundries Amount $	Sundries Account	GST paid $	Accounts payable control $

General Journal

Date	Particulars	Debit $	Credit $

Ex. 5.11 (a)

Stewart Distributors
Cash Payments Journal

Date	Particulars	Ref	Accounts payable control $	Sundries Amount $	Sundries Account	GST paid $	Bank $
						.	

Ex. 5.11 (b)

Stewart Distributors
General Ledger
Motor Vehicles – at Cost Account

Date	Particulars	Fol	Debit $	Credit $	Balance $

Motor Vehicle Registration and Insurance Account

Date	Particulars	Fol	Debit $	Credit $	Balance $

Motor Vehicle Repairs Account

Date	Particulars	Fol	Debit $	Credit $	Balance $

Depreciation – Motor Vehicles Account

Date	Particulars	Fol	Debit $	Credit $	Balance $

Ex. 5.11 (b)

Stewart Distributors
General Ledger

Accumulated Depreciation – Motor Vehicles Account

Date	Particulars	Fol	Debit $	Credit $	Balance $

Sale of Non-Current Assets Account

Date	Particulars	Fol	Debit $	Credit $	Balance $

Profit on Sale of Motor Vehicles Account

Date	Particulars	Fol	Debit $	Credit $	Balance $

Ex. 5.12 (a) Solution in textbook.

Nicholas Manufacturing
Purchases Journal

Date	Creditor	Ref	Purchases $	Sundries Amount $	Sundries Account	GST paid $	Accounts payable control $

Cash Payments Journal

Date	Particulars	Ref	Accounts payable control $	Sundries Amount $	Sundries Account	GST paid $	Bank $

General Journal

Date	Particulars	Debit $	Credit $

Ex. 5.12 (b) Solution in textbook.

Nicholas Industries
General Ledger
Motor Vehicles – at Cost Account

Date	Particulars	Fol	Debit $	Credit $	Balance $

Motor Vehicles Registration and Insurance Account

Date	Particulars	Fol	Debit $	Credit $	Balance $

Motor Vehicles Repairs Account

Date	Particulars	Fol	Debit $	Credit $	Balance $

Depreciation – Motor Vehicles Account

Date	Particulars	Fol	Debit $	Credit $	Balance $

Accumulated Depreciation – Motor Vehicles Account

Date	Particulars	Fol	Debit $	Credit $	Balance $

Ex. 5.12 (b) Solution in textbook.

Nicholas Industries
General Ledger
Sale of Non-Current Assets Account

Date	Particulars	Fol	Debit $	Credit $	Balance $

Profit on Sale Motor Vehicle Account

Date	Particulars	Fol	Debit $	Credit $	Balance $

Workings – calculation of depreciation

_____

_____

_____

_____

_____

_____

_____

_____

_____

_____

_____

_____

_____

_____

_____

_____

_____

_____

_____

_____

_____

_____

_____

Ex. 5.13

Moroney Industries
Purchases Journal

Date	Creditor	Ref	Purchases $	Sundries Amount $	Sundries Account	GST paid $	Accounts payable control $

Cash Payments Journal

Date	Particulars	Ref	Accounts payable control	Sundries Amount	Sundries Account	GST paid	Bank

Cash Receipts Journal

Date	Particulars	Ref	Accounts receivable control	Sundries Amount	Sundries Account	GST collected	Bank

General Journal

Date	Particulars	Debit $	Credit $

Ex. 5.14   Solution in textbook.

Alpha Sales
General Ledger
Motor Vehicles – at Cost Account

Date	Particulars	Fol	Debit $	Credit $	Balance $

Motor Vehicles Registration and Insurance Account

Date	Particulars	Fol	Debit $	Credit $	Balance $

Motor Vehicles Repairs Account

Date	Particulars	Fol	Debit $	Credit $	Balance $

Depreciation – Motor Vehicles Account

Date	Particulars	Fol	Debit $	Credit $	Balance $

Accumulated Depreciation – Motor Vehicles Account

Date	Particulars	Fol	Debit $	Credit $	Balance $

Ex. 5.14   Solution in textbook.

Alpha Sales
General Ledger
Sale of Non-current Assets Account

Date	Particulars	Fol	Debit $	Credit $	Balance $

Profit on Sale of Motor Vehicle Account

Date	Particulars	Fol	Debit $	Credit $	Balance $

Workings – calculation of depreciation

_____

_____

_____

_____

_____

_____

_____

_____

_____

_____

_____

Ex. 5.15 (a)

Waters Edge Industries
Purchases Journal

Date	Creditor	Ref	Purchases $	Sundries Amount $	Sundries Account	GST paid $	Accounts payable control $

Cash Payments Journal

Date	Particulars	Ref	Accounts payable control $	Sundries Amount $	Sundries Account	GST paid $	Bank $

Cash Receipts Journal

Date	Particulars	Ref	Accounts receivable control	Sundries Amount	Sundries Account	GST collected	Bank

General Journal

Date	Particulars	Debit $	Credit $

Ex. 5.15 (a)

Waters Edge Industries
General Journal

Date	Particulars	Debit $	Credit $

Depreciation Holden van BTF945 to date of disposal

Depreciation at 30 June 2018

Ex. 5.15 (b)

Waters Edge Industries
General Ledger
Motor Vehicles – at Cost Account

Date	Particulars	Fol	Debit $	Credit $	Balance $

Accumulated Depreciation – Motor Vehicles Account

Date	Particulars	Fol	Debit $	Credit $	Balance $

Depreciation – Motor Vehicles Account

Date	Particulars	Fol	Debit $	Credit $	Balance $

* Refer next page for calculation for depreciation on 30/6/18
Sale of Non-current Assets Account

Date	Particulars	Fol	Debit $	Credit $	Balance $

Ex. 5.15 (b)

Waters Edge Industries
General Ledger
Loss on Sale of Motor Vehicle Account

Date	Particulars	Fol	Debit $	Credit $	Balance $

Profit on Sale of Motor Vehicle Account

Date	Particulars	Fol	Debit $	Credit $	Balance $

Motor Vehicle Registration and Insurance Account

Date	Particulars	Fol	Debit $	Credit $	Balance $

Motor Vehicle Repairs Account

Date	Particulars	Fol	Debit $	Credit $	Balance $

Ex. 5.16

Acme Co
Cash Payments Journal

Date	Particular	Ref	Accounts payable control	Sundries Amount	Sundries Account	GST paid	Bank

Purchases Journal

Date	Creditor	Ref	Purchases	Sundries Amount	Sundries Account	GST paid	Accounts payable control

General Journal

Date	Particulars	Debit $	Credit $

Ex. 5.16

Workings – calculation of depreciation

Depreciation at 30 June 2020

_____

_____

_____

_____

_____

_____

_____

_____

Depreciation on model 310 photocopier to date of disposal

_____

_____

_____

_____

_____

_____

_____

_____

Accumulated depreciation of model 310 photocopier at date of disposal

_____

_____

_____

_____

_____

Ex. 5.17

Jeni's Diner
General Journal

Date	Particulars	Debit $	Credit $

Ex. 5.18 (a) Solution in textbook.

Neville's Engine Reconditioning
General Journal

Date	Particulars	Debit $	Credit $

Cash Payments Journal

Date	Particulars	Ref	Accounts payable control $	Sundries Amount $	Account	GST paid $	Bank $

Ex. 5.18 (b) Solution in textbook.

Neville's Engine Reconditioning
General Ledger
Workshop Equipment – at Cost Account

Date	Particulars	Fol	Debit $	Credit $	Balance $

Depreciation – Workshop Equipment Account

Date	Particulars	Fol	Debit $	Credit $	Balance $

Accumulated Depreciation – Workshop Equipment Account

Date	Particulars	Fol	Debit $	Credit $	Balance $

Loss on Scrapping of Workshop Equipment Account

Date	Particulars	Fol	Debit $	Credit $	Balance $

Workings – calculation of depreciation on the hoist to date of disposal

_____

_____

Ex. 5.19   Nature and purpose of an asset register.

_____

_____

_____

_____

_____

Ex. 5.20   Role of an asset register in an accounting system.

_____

_____

_____

_____

_____

_____

Ex. 5.21 (a)

Grant Tanner

Asset Register Card							
Item			General Ledger account				
Supplier			Depreciation – Method				
Serial No.			Depreciation – Rate % p.a.				
Est. life			Other details				
Location							
Financial History							
Date	Particulars	Asset			Accumulated depreciation			Carrying
		Dr	Cr	Balance	Dr	Cr	Balance	amount
		$	$	$	$	$	$	$

Asset Register Card							
Item			General Ledger account				
Supplier			Depreciation – Method				
Serial No.			Depreciation – Rate % p.a.				
Est. life			Other details				
Location							
Financial History							
Date	Particulars	Asset			Accumulated depreciation			Carrying
		Dr	Cr	Balance	Dr	Cr	Balance	amount
		$	$	$	$	$	$	$

Ex. 5.21 (a)

Grant Tanner

Asset Register Card							
Item		General Ledger account					
Supplier		Depreciation – Method					
Serial No.		Depreciation – Rate % p.a.					
Est. life		Other details					
Location							
Financial History							
Date	Particulars	Asset			Accumulated depreciation			Carrying amount
		Dr	Cr	Balance	Dr	Cr	Balance	
		$	$	$	$	$	$	$

Ex. 5.21 (b)

Grant Tanner, Builder
Statement of financial position as at 30 June 2017 (extract)

_____

_____

_____

_____

_____

_____

_____

Grant Tanner, Builder
Statement of financial position as at 30 June 2019 (extract)

_____

_____

_____

_____

_____

_____

_____

Ex. 5.22   Solution in textbook.

Tomkinson Industries

Asset Register Card							
Item			General Ledger account				
Supplier			Depreciation – Method				
Serial No.			Depreciation – Rate % p.a.				
Est. life			Other details				
Location							

		Financial History					
Date	Particulars	Asset			Accumulated depreciation		Carrying
		Dr	Cr	Balance	Dr	Cr	Balance	amount
		$	$	$	$	$	$	$

Asset Register Card (reverse side)			
Record of Repairs and Maintenance			
Date	Supplier	Nature of repairs	Amount
			$

Asset Register Card							
Item			General Ledger account				
Supplier			Depreciation – Method				
Serial No.			Depreciation – Rate % p.a.				
Est. life			Other details				
Location							

		Financial History					
Date	Particulars	Asset			Accumulated depreciation		Carrying
		Dr	Cr	Balance	Dr	Cr	Balance	amount
		$	$	$	$	$	$	$

Asset Register Card (reverse side)			
Record of Repairs and Maintenance			
Date	Supplier	Nature of repairs	Amount
			$

Ex. 5.23

Plastic Products

Asset Register Card							
Item		General Ledger account					
Supplier		Depreciation – Method					
Serial No.		Depreciation – Rate % p.a.					
Est. life		Other details					
Location							

		Financial History					
Date	Particulars	Asset			Accumulated depreciation			Carrying amount
		Dr	Cr	Balance	Dr	Cr	Balance	
		$	$	$	$	$	$	$

Asset Register Card (reverse side)			
Record of Repairs and Maintenance			
Date	Supplier	Nature of repairs	Amount
			$

Ex. 5.24

Boris Builders

Asset Register Card							
Item			General Ledger account				
Supplier			Depreciation – Method				
Reg. No.			Depreciation – Rate % p.a.				
Est. life			Other details				
Location							
Financial History							
Date	Particulars	Asset			Accumulated depreciation			Carrying
		Dr	Cr	Balance	Dr	Cr	Balance	amount
		$	$	$	$	$	$	$

Asset Register Card (reverse side)			
Record of Repairs and Maintenance			
Date	Supplier	Nature of repairs	Amount
			$

Asset Register Card							
Item			General Ledger account				
Supplier			Depreciation – Method				
Reg. No.			Depreciation – Rate % p.a.				
Est. life			Other details				
Location							
Financial History							
Date	Particulars	Asset			Accumulated depreciation			Carrying
		Dr	Cr	Balance	Dr	Cr	Balance	amount
		$	$	$	$	$	$	$

Asset Register Card (reverse side)			
Record of Repairs and Maintenance			
Date	Supplier	Nature of repairs	Amount
			$

Ex. 5.25   Solution in textbook.

Andrews Enterprises
General Ledger
Plant and Equipment – at Cost Account

Date	Particulars	Fol	Debit $	Credit $	Balance $

Depreciation – Plant and Equipment Account

Date	Particulars	Fol	Debit $	Credit $	Balance $

Accumulated Depreciation – Plant and Equipment Account

Date	Particulars	Fol	Debit $	Credit $	Balance $

Equipment Repairs Account

Date	Particulars	Fol	Debit $	Credit $	Balance $

Loss on Scrapping of Plant and Equipment Account

Date	Particulars	Fol	Debit $	Credit $	Balance $

Workings – calculation of depreciation
See next page

Ex. 5.25 **Solution in textbook.**

Andrews Enterprises

Workings – calculation of depreciation
Year ended 30 June 2019

_____

_____

_____

_____

_____

1 July 2019 to September 2019 – lathe 323

_____

_____

_____

_____

Lathe 323 – accumulated depreciation to date of scrapping

_____

_____

_____

_____

_____

_____

_____

_____

_____

Year ended 30 June 2020

_____

_____

_____

_____

_____

_____

_____

Ex. 5.26 (a)

Derek's Floor Coverings

Asset Register Card							
Item			General Ledger account				
Supplier			Depreciation – Method				
Reg. No.			Depreciation – Rate % p.a.				
Est. life			Other details				
Location							

		Financial History						
Date	Particulars	Asset			Accumulated depreciation			Carrying amount
		Dr	Cr	Balance	Dr	Cr	Balance	
		$	$	$	$	$	$	$

Asset Register Card (reverse side)			
Record of Repairs and Maintenance			
Date	Supplier	Nature of repairs	Amount
			$

Workings – calculation of depreciation

Year ended 30 June 2017

_____

_____

_____

_____

_____

_____

_____

Ex. 5.26 (b)

Derek's Floor Coverings
Purchases Journal

Date	Creditor	Ref	Purchases $	Sundries Amount $	Sundries Account	GST paid $	Accounts payable control $

Cash Payments Journal

Date	Particulars	Ref	Accounts payable control $	Sundries Amount $	Sundries Account	GST paid $	Bank $

Cash Receipts Journal

Date	Particulars	Ref	Accounts Receivable Control $	Sundries Amount $	Sundries Account	GST collected $	Bank $

General Journal

Date	Particulars	Debit $	Credit $

Ex. 5.26 (b)

Derek's Floor Coverings
General Journal

Date	Particulars	Debit $	Credit $

Calculation of depreciation at 30 June 2017

_____

_____

_____

_____

_____

_____

_____

_____

Ex. 5.26 (c)

Derek's Floor Coverings
General Ledger
Motor Vehicles – at Cost Account

Date	Particulars	Fol	Debit $	Credit $	Balance $

Depreciation – Motor Vehicles Account

Date	Particulars	Fol	Debit $	Credit $	Balance $

Accumulated Depreciation – Motor Vehicles Account

Date	Particulars	Fol	Debit $	Credit $	Balance $

Motor Vehicle Registration and Insurance Account

Date	Particulars	Fol	Debit $	Credit $	Balance $

Ex. 5.26 (c)

Derek's Floor Coverings
General Ledger
Motor Vehicle Repairs and Maintance Account

Date	Particulars	Fol	Debit $	Credit $	Balance $

Sale of Non-current Assets Account

Date	Particulars	Fol	Debit $	Credit $	Balance $

Loss on Sale of Motor Vehicle Account

Date	Particulars	Fol	Debit $	Credit $	Balance $

Ex. 5.27

Loo's Photo Bargain Mart
General Ledger
Photo Processing Equipment – at Cost Account

Date	Particulars	Fol	Debit $	Credit $	Balance $

Depreciation – Photo Processing Equipment Account

Date	Particulars	Fol	Debit $	Credit $	Balance $

Accumulated Depreciation – Photo Processing Equipment Account

Date	Particulars	Fol	Debit $	Credit $	Balance $

Chemicals Expense Account

Date	Particulars	Fol	Debit $	Credit $	Balance $

Equipment Repairs Account

Date	Particulars	Fol	Debit $	Credit $	Balance $

Ex. 5.27

Loo's Photo Bargain Mart
General Ledger
Sale of Non-current Assets Account

Date	Particulars	Fol	Debit $	Credit $	Balance $

Loss on Sale of Photo Processing Equipment Account

Date	Particulars	Fol	Debit $	Credit $	Balance $

Workings – calculation of depreciation
Depreciation at 30 June 2018

_____

_____

_____

_____

Depreciation of photo dryer to date of disposal

_____

_____

Accumulated depreciation of photo dryer at date of disposal

_____

_____

_____

_____

Ex. 5.28

Diddles Industries
Purchases Journal

Date	Creditor	Ref	Purchases $	Sundries Amount $	Sundries Account	GST paid $	Accounts payable control $

Cash Payments Journal

Date	Particulars	Ref	Accounts payable control $	Sundries Amount $	Sundries Account	GST paid $	Bank $

General Journal

Date	Particulars	Debit $	Credit $

Ex. 5.28

Diddles Industries

Calculations – Depreciation at 30 June 2018

_____

_____

_____

_____

_____

_____

_____

_____

_____

_____

_____

Ex. 5.29   Solution in textbook.

Laurie Driver
Asset Register Reconciliation Report for year ended 30 June 2018

Asset ID No	Asset description	Cost $	Depreciation y/e 30/6/18 $	Accumulated depreciation $
Total as per General Ledger accounts:				
Motor Vehicles – at Cost				
Depreciation – Motor Vehicles				
Accumulated Depreciation – Motor Vehicles				
Total as per General Ledger accounts:				
Office Equipment – at Cost				
Depreciation – Office Equipment				
Accumulated Depreciation – Office Equipment				
Total as per General Ledger accounts:				
Furniture and Fittings – at Cost				
Depreciation – Furniture and Fittings				
Accumulated Depreciation – Furniture and Fittings				

Ex. 5.30   Solution in textbook.

Michael Ellis Industries

(a)   **General Journal**

Date	Particulars	Debit $	Credit $

(b)   **Cash Payments Journal (simplified)**

Date	Particulars	Ref	Accounts payable control $	Sundries Amount $	Sundries Account	GST paid $	Bank $

(c)   **General Journal**

Date	Particulars	Debit $	Credit $

Workings – calculation of annual depreciation

_____

_____

_____

_____

_____

_____

_____

Ex. 5.31

Esnouf Constructions

(a)

General Journal

Date	Particulars	Debit $	Credit $

(b)

Cash Payments Journal

Date	Particulars	Ref	Accounts payable control $	Sundries Amount $	Sundries Account	GST paid $	Bank $

(c)

General Journal

Date	Particulars	Debit $	Credit $

Workings – calculation of annual depreciation

_____

_____

_____

_____